YORK NOTES

Philip Larkin
The Whitsun Weddings and Selected Poems

Notes by David Punter

The right of David Punter to be identified as Author of this work has been asserted by him in accordance with the Copyright, Designs and Patents Act 1988

© Faber and Faber Ltd

Extracts from Philip Larkin, Collected Poems reproduced with permission of the publishers, Faber and Faber Ltd.

YORK PRESS
322 Old Brompton Road, London SW5 9JH

PEARSON EDUCATION LIMITED
Edinburgh Gate, Harlow,
Essex CM20 2JE, United Kingdom
Associated companies, branches and representatives throughout the world

© Librairie du Liban *Publishers* 2003

All rights reserved. No part of this publication may be reproduced, stored in a retrieval system, or transmitted in any form or by any means, electronic, mechanical, photocopying, recording, or otherwise, without either the prior written permission of the Publishers or a licence permitting restricted copying in the United Kingdom issued by the Copyright Licensing Agency Ltd, 90 Tottenham Court Road, London W1T 4LP

First published 2003
14

ISBN: 978-0-582-77229-8

Designed by Vicki Pacey
Typeset by Land & Unwin (
Printed in Great Britain by A
(EPC/10)

TORFAEN COUNTY BOROUGH BWRDEISTREF SIROL TORFAEN	
01683591	
Askews & Holts	19-Oct-2016
821.914	£7.99

Contents

PART ONE

INTRODUCTION   How to Study a Poem   5
Reading Philip Larkin's Poetry   6

PART TWO

COMMENTARIES   Note on the Text   8
Detailed Commentaries   9
    Wedding-Wind   9
    Next, Please   10
    Days   12
    Toads   15
    Water   17
    Church Going   19
    Mr Bleaney   22
    An Arundel Tomb   24
    The Whitsun Weddings   27
    Self's the Man   29
    Home is so Sad   31
    Faith Healing   33
    Talking in Bed   35
    Take One Home for the Kiddies   36
    A Study of Reading Habits   37
    The Large Cool Store   39
    Nothing To Be Said   42
    Wild Oats   43
    Essential Beauty   46
    Sunny Prestatyn   48
    Dockery and Son   50
    High Windows   53
    Annus Mirabilis   55
    Sad Steps   56
    The Explosion   59
    The Card-Players   60
    This Be The Verse   62
    Going, Going   64
    The Building   67
    Aubade   70

PART THREE

EXTENDED COMMENTARIES
    Poem 1 – Ambulances   72
    Poem 2 – Here   75
    Poem 3 – Toads Revisited   78

PART FOUR

CRITICAL APPROACHES
    Themes   82
        The Poetic Persona   82
        Everyday Life   83
        Human Emotions   84
        Loneliness and Loss   85
        Death   86
    Language and Style   88
    Imagery and Symbolism   92

PART FIVE

BACKGROUND   The Life of Philip Larkin   96
    Historical & Literary Background   97
        The Movement   97
        Ted Hughes   98
        Angry Young Men   98
        Britain in the 1960s and beyond   99
    Literary Influences   100

PART SIX

CRITICAL HISTORY AND FURTHER READING
    Contemporary Criticism   102
    Posthumous Criticism   103
    Poststructuralist Criticism   104
    Further Reading   106

Chronology   108
Literary Terms   113
Author of these Notes   116

Part One

Introduction

How to study a poem

Studying a poem on your own requires self-discipline and a carefully thought-out work plan in order to be effective.

- You will need to read the poem more than once. Start by reading it quickly for pleasure, then read it slowly and thoroughly.
- Look up all the words which you do not know. Some may have more than one meaning so note them. They may be intended to be ambiguous.
- On your second reading make detailed notes on the plot, characters and themes of the poem. Further readings will generate new ideas and help you to memorise the details.
- Think about how the poem is narrated. From whose point of view are the events described? Does your response to the narrator change at all in the course of the poem?
- The main character is the narrator, but what about the others? Do they develop? Do you only ever see them from the narrator's point of view?
- Identify what styles of language are used in the poem.
- Assess what the main arguments are in the poem. Who are the narrator's main opponents? Are their views ever fairly presented?
- Are words, images or incidents repeated so as to give the work a pattern? Do such patterns help you to understand the poem's themes?
- What is the effect of the poem's ending? Is the action completed and closed, or left incomplete and open?
- Does the poem present a world or point of view of which you are meant to approve?
- Cite exact sources for all quotations, whether from the text itself or from critical commentaries. Wherever possible find your own examples from the poem to back up your opinions.
- Always express your ideas in your own words.

These York Notes offer an introduction to Philip Larkin's poetry and cannot substitute for close reading of the text and the study of secondary sources.

Reading Philip Larkin's Poetry

At the time of his death in 1985, Philip Larkin was widely regarded as the most significant poet of post-war England. He had published only four substantial volumes of poetry, as well as two early novels and some essays, and the editor of his *Collected Poems* has been able to find little other work of substance. Yet the last three of his books of poetry – *The Less Deceived* (1955), *The Whitsun Weddings* (1964) and *High Windows* (1974) – demonstrate very clearly that Larkin was a master of his art. These poems are concise, elegantly and economically descriptive, versatile in their use of forms, endlessly suggestive of deeper resonances in the scenes they paint. Perhaps more than this, it became evident from the reception of his poetry that Larkin was far more than a craftsman: there was a profound affinity between the characteristic moods and tones of his poetry and the currents of feeling running through England itself in the forty years of his writing career.

Larkin's poetic career spanned a period of enormous changes in English society, from the war through to the 1970s; but we find quite few poems of his which refer directly to historical or social events. The influence of English social life on his work, while extremely strong, has to be seen in broader terms than that. For Larkin always had an impressive knowledge of ordinary life as it is lived by millions of English people. He was familiar with the high street shops; he was familiar with the weather; he was familiar with the maxims and sayings by which people actually govern their lives. In other words, he preferred to describe life as it is lived rather than to measure life by unattainable ideals, although a certain **irony** about these ideals is omnipresent in his poetry.

Larkin was a poet under nobody's influence. One of his great strengths was his apparently almost unthinking alertness to contemporary conversational tones and rhythms; in his poems he rarely pontificates, and he never settles for the easy answer. His problem, perhaps – and it might in part account for the slightness of his output – lay in finding those moments when **colloquial** thought, feeling and language can come together in an unstrained way with the drive for formality which structures his poems. When this is achieved, it is a testimony not only to his own poetic power and prodigious reading but also to the ear for a poetic phrase which is, one should say, not the province of the poet alone. For after all, there is great poetic skill in old sayings, proverbs, in people's everyday ways of putting things; it is this unthought skill which Larkin was able to tune in to and raise to another notch without sacrificing the common applicability of age-old truths.

None of this is to suggest that Larkin was merely a populist poet, and neither was he in any sense a celebratory one; indeed, some of the emotions and social feelings he reveals are problematic and, in some ways, deeply unpalatable, and his sense of mortality is urgent to the point of obsession. Nonetheless, even in these areas it remains apparent that he tapped into and in some sense represented a Zeitgeist, the spirit of an age. That such a position should entail contact with the seamier sides of life as well as with moments of sudden, transcending beauty is essential to Larkin's perception and portrayal of the world around him.

PART TWO

COMMENTARIES

NOTE ON THE TEXT

With a poet as careful as Larkin, there are no obvious problems with the text. These Notes are based on Philip Larkin's *Collected Poems*, edited with an introduction by Anthony Thwaite (Faber and Faber, 1988), which contains all of Larkin's published poems, with a selection of juvenilia. In the Commentaries that follow, poems are discussed in the order in which they appear in this volume. There are no significant discrepancies between these versions and those that appeared in the individual volumes.

In these York Notes, the focus is on thirty poems. The majority – seventeen – are from *The Whitsun Weddings*; but also included are four poems ('Wedding-Wind', 'Next, Please', 'Toads' and 'Church Going') from *The Less Deceived*; eight ('High Windows', 'Annus Mirabilis', 'Sad Steps', 'The Explosion', 'The Card-Players', 'This Be The Verse', 'Going, Going' and 'The Building') from *High Windows*; and one later poem, 'Aubade', which appeared, after the publication of the last of these volumes, in *The Times Literary Supplement* in 1977.

The Whitsun Weddings, the central volume with which these Notes is concerned, contains thirty-two poems. It would be convenient if one could isolate *The Whitsun Weddings* from the rest of Larkin's work and say that it focuses on specific themes, or represents a particular stage in his writing, but with Larkin matters are not quite like that. The poem 'The Whitsun Weddings' itself, to be sure, crystallises a particular aspect of his perception; but otherwise one would have to say that the themes and styles of the volume run also through *The Less Deceived* and *High Windows*. Those themes include mortality; the fear of ageing; the delusions of desire; vulnerabilty and ill-health; and what it means to live one's life alone. The Commentaries below will pick up on some of these themes in the poems from *The Whitsun Weddings*; but, by including poems from the other major volumes, we may see how they run right through Larkin's poetic corpus.

Detailed Commentaries

Wedding-Wind   (from *The Less Deceived*)

A just-married young woman looks back on her wedding and muses on her fortune and her married state

The persona of this poem is a woman: a young woman, a farm girl perhaps. It is the day after her wedding; in the first verse paragraph she takes us back to her wedding day and wedding night, and to her new husband. Very gently in this paragraph we are introduced to her happiness and sense of fulfilment at being married and her sense of loss when her new husband is absent even for a short time. When she thinks about the horses, restless because of the wind, it is only to contrast that restlessness with her own peace and contentment.

In the second paragraph, on the surface all is back to normal again; there are the effects of the rain to be dealt with, the chickens to be fed. But in the midst of this normality the wind encourages in her a reverie, in which she listens in her mind to the wind and thinks of it as a force which is comparable to the all-changing joy she feels. Although there is peace, there is also the underlying feeling that everything has altered, that her new condition is so filled with joy that it seems as though it might transcend death itself. At the end she offers up a kind of hymn of praise to the powers which have allowed her this life-altering experience, an experience which, she feels, will never leave her.

> Larkin takes great care to introduce us to the simplicity of this young woman: the phrase 'That he must go and shut it' is slightly colloquial; the phrase 'I was sad' moves by its clarity and the directness of feeling it expresses.

> At the same time, the imagery itself is not simple. The central image of the wind might perhaps remind us of the wind which 'long has raved unnoticed' in Coleridge's 'Dejection: An Ode', or of Shelley's 'Ode to the West Wind'. It goes through three distinct stages. In the first paragraph we are invited to experience the wind literally and its power to disturb yet also to reassure her in her secure happiness, which she wishes all creatures to share. Her reverie starts with 'All is the wind', reminding us that the wind is a greater and wider power than that of the merely human. In the end we are all at the mercy of the wind, although in her case the wind is indeed merciful.

Wedding-wind

The most complex part of the image are the lines 18–20. Might the wind, Larkin asks, be too strong for us? Or might we see it as a unifying force, as something which makes sense of all our actions, even if we cannot ourselves understand them? And there is also a hint of the beads of the rosary, which moves us on to the 'thanksgiving' mood of the final lines.

Those final lines are biblical in their feel, but not insistently so; we are invited to think about the simple religion which this woman has absorbed, which is compounded of Christianity and an older, nature-based sense of awe. The world of Thomas Hardy, always a formidable influence on English poetry in the twentieth century, can be sensed throughout.

For all the sense of peace, there is also an undertone of disturbance in the poem. The woman's happiness reminds her of the frailty of the human; it is as though in her simplicity she is content to resign herself to a higher power, trusting and pliant, and to see herself as akin to the 'cattle'. Yet for all that she cannot see the future clearly; she is too much under the spell of this almost magical process of transformation to know what will come next. The word 'thrashing' and the phrase 'Shall I be let to sleep' remind us that powers which can seem to be beneficial also constitute an exposure to forces immeasurably greater than ourselves; and who can know what the consequences of this may be?

ravelled one of the rare words in the English language which also means its own opposite: 'entangled' and 'disentangled'
bodying-forth giving a shape to, incarnating

Next, please (FROM *The Less Deceived*)

This is a poem about postponement and anticipation; about how we spend our lives waiting for the next thing to happen and expecting good fortune. Instead, Larkin claims, in the process we waste our lives; the only real news coming is the news of our death

The 'bad habits of expectancy' which Larkin refers to in the first stanza are simply a way of occluding the present by staking all our hopes on the future, on the idea that things will get better. 'Something', he says, 'is always approaching': we are awaiting our next pay packet or salary cheque, or the hope of meeting the 'right person', or some change that will alter our lives for ever.

But this resting of our hopes in the future merely 'leaves us holding wretched stalks / Of disappointment'; those things that we expect never seem really to get closer, there is something that stops them at every turn. As in so many others of his poems, Larkin is here thinking about the nature of desire, about how our wishes can never be fully satisfied; of the way in which as soon as one desire is fulfilled we move on to the next, leaving ourselves in a constant state of dissatisfaction and disappointment.

Another way of putting this is to say that there is never an isolable present moment; no sooner have we achieved something than it inexorably becomes part of the past ('No sooner present than it turns to past') and thus becomes devalued, robbed of the satisfaction we imagined it should have provided.

Our hopes, we suppose, are even sanctioned by religion: that which we wait for we wait for 'devoutly', as believers in the future, in the possible upturn of fate, even perhaps in a just God; but, the poet says, in this again we are wrong – nothing is promised to us, with one exception, the great exception of death. Death is, of course, not what we anticipate – in the sense that we do not hope for it – but then, what we have to learn is that it is not within the power of our own agency to produce the future, it is rather that the future has its own designs – or, indeed, its single design – upon us, and in this way and this way only it cannot and will not be deflected.

> The whole poem is beautifully structured around a single stream of imagery. The protagonist is pictured as 'Watching from a bluff', from a headland or cliff, while a 'Sparkling armada of promises' comes ever closer; the imagery is drawn from a whole history of treasure-seeking, the essentially imperial idea that vast wealth can be brought home from foreign parts. Although the 'big approach' of each ship seems inevitable, and although we can see their flags, ropework, brasswork and figureheads distinctly, nonetheless they are not really drawing closer. They will never anchor or unload, and instead they will be replaced – replaced by the extraordinary image that dominates the final stanza of the poem.

Before turning to that closing image – 'closing' in all senses of the word – it is perhaps worth noticing Larkin's characteristic deprecatory trademark, the description of the figureheads as having 'golden tits': that slippage into vulgarity is also relevant to the whole texture and content of the poem, insofar as the very investment of all our hopes in the future is itself a kind of vulgarisation, a derogation from the potential of the present.

The final image, though, has nothing of vulgarity about it; on the contrary it is the very acme of dignity, and it is partly from this, from the ineluctable trajectory of this ship of death, that it derives its enormous power. This ship brings no wealth or fortune, no treasure, no goods of any kind; instead, what it tows behind it is 'A huge and birdless silence', the end to all our hopes and indeed all our fears, and the end also of words, of language, of poetry; the end, too, of humanity itself as 'No waters breed'. The image speaks of our own death as individuals but also carries intimations of the eventual extinction of the species, a fate which is beyond both our imagining and our control and which therefore proves all those efforts at control fruitless. All our hopes for future improvement are shown to be futile.

armada fleet of ships
balks prevents or obstructs
prinked polished to perfection
heave to drop anchor, stop
unfamiliar something unknown to us, here also perhaps carrying a sense of the witch's 'familiar', her accompanying spirit

DAYS (FROM THE WHITSUN WEDDINGS)

Addresses issues of mortality, illness and death in a form of apparently remarkable simplicity

This short and enigmatic poem takes a very simple word, and a very simple notion, 'days' – one which, perhaps, we never ordinarily think about at all – and inspects it. No story is told here, and we have no characters to connect with; instead we have a brief contemplation and one which, at first glance, may seem deeply inconclusive.

This very short poem, which uses extremely simple language, nevertheless demonstrates, as we look at it carefully, considerable skill and also an interesting approach to vital matters of life and death. It is a good poem on which to attempt a line-by-line analysis.

LINE 1: The question sounds childlike; we almost expect 'mummy' to appear at the end of the line, as if the question itself could only be put by somebody to whom the very word 'days' is new – a child who, for example, has just come across it for the first time in an alphabet book.

LINE 2: The concept here is one of home, of homeliness, of feeling at home in the world. In the brightness of daylight we feel that we can understand things, that a straightforward, clear account of the world makes sense. Already perhaps we can hear the other, unasked question: what, then, of nights? If days are the sources of our reassurance of life, what then of darkness, of that which we cannot understand?

LINE 3: We sense here a possible reply by the parent to the child. Of course we know that it is not precisely the case that days wake us; but this answer, the poet implies, will perhaps suffice for the child, for somebody to whom the whole world is still a mystery to be enjoyed.

LINE 4: This line contains an ambiguity. On the surface it means the same as 'Time and time again'; but the separate phrase 'time over' carries an implication of the end of this safe world of days without end.

LINE 5: Again this carries the tone of the parent answering the child; and perhaps by this time we may sense that this is a drama of question and answer which is also being enacted *within* an individual. The innocence of the questioning represents a desire to be satisfied by simplicity, although the happiness spoken of may in fact prove elusive.

LINE 6: This line moves us on from the question-and-answer format, as though the voice of the parent is now asking itself a question. As we reassure our children of life, light, happiness, perhaps we also ask ourselves what is the 'other side' of days.

The break between the two stanzas marks a change: a change of mood from certainty to puzzlement, and also a change of vocabulary such that the simple monosyllables which signify an unchanging world are replaced by two-syllable words like 'question', 'doctor', 'Running', which increase the urgency of the poem and suggest to us the deeper problems of time and mortality which cannot be answered by just referring to life as consisting of an endless succession of days.

LINE 7: The initial 'Ah' also marks this break; rather than briskly answering questions, the poetic voice is now moving further into reverie. 'Solving', as well as meaning 'finding a solution to', carries a hint of 'dissolving', so that we see that the wider questions require us to dissolve the apparent certainties of the first stanza.

LINE 8: Why the priest and the doctor? They are the people who are concerned with the real problems of mortality: with the health and survival of the soul, with the health of the body; in short, with death.

LINE 9: This is, of course, a literal reference to the priest's cassock, to the doctor's white coat. But we sense in these 'long coats' also the force of a symbol, although, like all symbols, it may be difficult to pin down. We are here being referred back to the world of the child, but now in a frightening way: to the sense a child may have that somebody in a 'long coat' may represent problems beyond control, beyond understanding.

LINE 10: The fields are the bright, sunlit fields of day; the priest and the doctor spoil this perfect picture. They also bring into a peaceful scene a note of urgency, the urgency which follows from our gradual recognition – enacted throughout the poem – of the superior power of death, the decay of the body, and the need to find an answer, beyond the grave, to the initial questions and particularly to the question which occurs around the midpoint of the poem, 'Where can we live but days?' When days run out, shall we find ourselves still living? And in what way?

T OADS   (FROM THE LESS DECEIVED)

A complex meditation on work and desire, on the things we take for granted and the satisfactions that elude us

As in other poems, Larkin takes on the **persona** of the common man, asking questions about things which we take for granted. We might assume that life consists mainly of working, in this case six days a week – or perhaps the sixth is spent worrying about work! But why should this be the case? Might there not be a better way to live?

The persona sees other people, people on the fringes of society, living without this compulsion to work in the usual sense of the term: gypsies, academics – perhaps, by implication, poets. By living in this way people do not get rich, but they survive.

But how, he asks, can he get himself into this position? So many of us are bound into our jobs, our habits of life. We fear for the future; we fear what will happen to us if at the end of the day we do not have a pension on which to fall back.

We must conclude, then, that this compulsion to work, to conform to the norms of society, is not merely something imposed from the outside, something which squats like a toad on our deeper wishes for freedom, unconventionality; instead it is something which lives inside ourselves, something which we have *internalised*; it 'Squats in me, too'. It is nonetheless perceived as inevitable; the fear embodied in 'hard luck' and the coldness of 'snow' represent the internal pressures which keep us from any attempt to break free.

There may be *other* people who can gratify their desires, get 'The fame and the girl and the money' without working; but we can never be like them. What we are left with instead is the perpetual compromise embodied in the last stanza, for although Larkin seems positive at this point, we are invited to see an irony here, a way in which we all persuade ourselves, after all, that the conventional lives we lead are more satisfying and less risky than the other lives which, from time to time, we may find ourselves envying.

The poem is called 'Toads', not 'Toad', and so it cannot refer only to the 'toad *work*' but must also refer to the way in which we ourselves become toadlike, unimaginative, weighed down by our bodies and by habit as we submit to these pressures.

The stanza form Larkin uses is jaunty, almost throwaway; it suggests an absence of deep thought, and this is because Larkin is here talking about the excuses we offer to ourselves to avoid thinking deeply about our situation. Although the persona may appear to value the lives of those outside the social pale, the terms he uses of them – 'lispers, / Losels, loblolly-men, louts' – simultaneously suggest that he avoids considering them as serious alternatives by despising them.

The word 'wit'/'wits' in stanzas one and three implicitly compares the 'wit' of the poet, or simply of the intelligent person, with the 'wits' of the person who has the perhaps innate skills to avoid the toad; but the comparison is **ironic**, so that in the end the poem appears to try to persuade us that real 'wit' or intelligence can only end up making us content with the way things are.

Notice the sudden changes of tone: for example, the language of 'pitchfork', 'brute', 'sickening', contrasted with the **colloquialism** of 'Just for paying a few bills'. From the beginning we are unsettled as to how seriously we should take the argument being advanced. The irony here is all-pervasive; we are invited to consider the opinion of the persona as representing a serious alternative while we can see that he is in fact prejudiced and timid.

Notice also the contempt in the fifth stanza. This persona is really one who scorns those who are beyond convention, and therefore it is not surprising that he cannot move beyond convention himself.

There is a considerable change of tone at the beginning of the seventh stanza, where we are made to feel the real sombreness of a life lived according to the dictates of the toad. But this moment of revelation and fear cannot be sustained by the persona, who needs to cheer himself up in the joking tones of stanza eight.

What, then, does the last stanza mean? Perhaps there is no definitive answer to this, but we could say that the 'one' and the 'other' are the two types of life being talked about, in which case the persona is concluding by saying that he has both of these kinds of life. But surely if this is true, then he only has the second kind of life, the life of 'toadlessness', *in his imagination*; and if that is true, does that make him timid, or self-deluding, or is he finally talking about the unavoidable ambiguity of being a poet, whose business it is to imagine but not to live out other people's lives?

lispers Larkin here implies homosexuals and poets in the same term, on the assumption that this bracketing is familiar to the presumed 'common man'
losels (*archaic*) rascals
loblolly-men a dialect word for louts
windfalls fruit blown down by the wind; also unexpected good luck
whippets extraordinarily thin racing dogs
the stuff / That dreams are made on a virtual quotation from Shakespeare, *The Tempest* IV.1.156–7
hunkers haunches
blarney an Irish word for cajole

WATER   (FROM THE WHITSUN WEDDINGS)

Larkin is not on the whole a poet whom one might call 'symbolist'; but this poem certainly develops a single symbol, the symbol of water, in puzzling ways and uses it to connect with questions of religious observance

The poem starts in a matter-of-fact fashion. Larkin writes as though the job he might be called upon to perform were that of a carpenter or plumber. But the job, although cast in terms of the construction industry, is to 'construct a religion'. The implications are complex: on the one hand, this notion could imply that all religions are 'constructed' – in other words, that they are quite literally fabrications – but it becomes increasingly clear as the poem goes on that there is potentially more to a religion than that.

He speaks, essentially, of the many uses to which water might be put – in the 'construction' of a religious observance, to be sure, but also by implication in the service of poetry. In putting forward these uses it is obvious that there is, one might say, a certain subtext because the Christian religion, at least, does make significant use of water. One might think of baptism as the prime example, but there is also the whole range of related uses for 'holy water', not to mention the episode in the Bible in which Jesus turns water to wine; the episode of walking on water; and there are, indeed, many more.

So one might not want to take the notion of 'constructing' a new religion quite at face value; perhaps what Larkin is talking about has at least as much to do with questions of how to imbue old symbols with greater value, with how to revitalise traditions which might have become moribund, lacking in energy and renewal.

> In the second stanza, he talks of 'fording'. The idea behind this is perhaps not unlike the theory of baptism, as marking a kind of transition between worlds, and also a dealing with the complexities of soul and body. But the term is a deliberately matter-of-fact one: Larkin is not thinking, one supposes, of grandiloquent episodes also involving water, such as the parting of the waters in the Bible, but of something more ordinary, more everyday, the possibility of finding 'dry, different clothes'. Nevertheless, insofar as baptism represents a form of rebirth, such a rebirth is also clearly in the poet's mind, a kind of shedding of old encumbrances with the attendant possibility of re-emerging in a different, transformed shape.

> With the image of 'sousing', however, the poem takes a different turn: instead of the comparatively measured idea of 'fording', we now have a far more 'furious' notion of what it might take to make a difference: not so much a gentle transmutation, more a violent sloughing off of a previous life, an event in which one is placed completely under the influence of some outside power, some incomprehensible 'devout drench' – which carries also the implications of liberating one from sickness, curing one of disease, which might be the disease of life itself.

> It is, however, the final stanza which – dare one say miraculously – stills the violence of this image and at the same time entirely overcomes the tentative **ironies** of the first two stanzas. Perhaps it is pointless to ask what this final stanza 'means'; it seems more to be an 'act', perhaps almost closer to Zen Buddhism than to Christianity, an act of sacrament in which the perfectly ordinary, exposed to a certain light, taken to a certain degree of belief and faith, can take on entirely different contours. Why the east? Perhaps this does indeed intensify the notion of something Buddhistic, although if so, it marks a point of reference that occurs nowhere else in Larkin's poetry. More

probably it refers us to the dawn, to the idea of a new beginning or awakening. The remainder of the image seems to have something to do with the possibility of both encompassing and focusing; with finding in the image of the glass of water and its constantly changing refractions some kind of correlative for a bringing of some form of order to chaos – perhaps, indeed, as a poem does.

Possibly, then, the peculiar place of this poem in Larkin's oeuvre might be as a kind of symbolic description of the act of poetry itself. Perhaps it offers a concept of a poem that can take 'any-angled light' – light falling from anywhere – and convert it into some notion of 'congregation', some notion whereby the poem itself is capable of forming its own community of readers, and thus acts as a focus for belief, understanding and emotion.

liturgy the words of a church service
sousing virtually synonymous with drenching, although with an added slang connotation of being drunk

CHURCH GOING   (FROM THE LESS DECEIVED)

A man out cycling comes into a church. Initially he is unimpressed – or refuses to be impressed – but as the poem goes on, his detachment is gradually affected by all that the church stands for

This is one of Larkin's most famous and complex poems, and in it he again assumes the persona of the common man trying to explain to himself some of the most commanding features of British culture, in this case the meaning of religious observance.

We are to picture him as a casual weekend cyclist who arrives at a church. In the first two stanzas he enters the church, not knowing quite how to behave; he knows that people remove their hats in churches, but since he has no hat he removes his cycle-clips instead. He can see the significant features of the building, knows which end is which, but he does not have the knowledge or the sensibility to enter deeply into this. Instead he does the things any tourist might do, and leaves none the wiser.

Or so it seems. In the third stanza we are told that this is not just a single event, that he has often felt compelled to visit churches in this way before. He begins to meditate, as before, on what use churches are now that established Christianity is in decay. Will churches become – or have they already become – museums whose real purpose is lost? Or will they, as he suggests in stanza four, become the haunt of latter-day witches? What strange people, he asks in stanza five, will eventually remain interested in churches, and how distant will their motives be from those which inspired the religion to which they were originally dedicated?

In stanza six he returns to his apparently uninformed stance, yet also suggests that, at least, the ceremonies of life, marriage and death retain, whether we know it or not, their overarching importance as markers of our lives. And in the final stanza he changes tone, to recognise in highly serious language that, no matter how decayed a church or religion itself may be, nevertheless it remains a kind of magnet for the more serious, profound aspects of our feelings – feelings which will never die and which may continue to need for their proper expression a 'serious house on serious earth', no matter how far our personal motives and capacities may have diverged from the original intent of the Church.

In the third stanza Larkin uses the phrase 'parchment, plate and pyx'. We might fairly ask: if he really is the common man of the persona, then how would he know about such erudite terms? This opens up the whole question of the relation between Larkin and his **persona**: to what extent is he adopting a pose of learning but **ironically** suggesting that the era in which learning is valued is at an end?

The poem is written in seven nine-line stanzas, with a very regular form. The typical line is an **iambic pentameter**. By using this line Larkin asserts his continuity with many other English poets, for this is the most frequent line-form in English-language poetry. Notice the rhyme scheme: we may formally describe it as ABABCADCD, but we also encounter within this structure many half-rhymes: that is, rhymes where the consonants match but the vowels although related are not identical: 'on'/'stone', 'stuff'/'off', and so forth.

Notice also how ably Larkin uses this complex versification to contain sentences of ordinary, even **colloquial, syntax**: for example, 'Someone would know: I don't'. In this way he manages to convey a double voice: the voice of the ordinary man, reflected in the sentence structure, alongside or set off against the voice of the poet, reflected in the verse form, rhyme and rhythm.

At the beginning of the fourth stanza Larkin elevates and mystifies his language. Why does he do this? He suggests, first, the connection of the Church with a cultural tradition; second, the poet's own access to such tradition; third, the way in which such tradition can appear in the contemporary world only in debased form; fourth, the way in which even an apparently uneducated persona, when in search of explanations or symbols, may inevitably turn to the past as a vehicle for myths, cultural values, the very language which we use in everyday speech.

The title 'Church Going' is ambiguous. It suggests the habit of going to church on Sundays, and it also suggests that the Church itself as an institution is 'going', both in the sense of vanishing and also in the sense that it is perhaps only the church which now marks our own 'going', our passing away.

Consider, as one small emblem of the technique Larkin uses, the phrase 'accoutred frowsty barn'. The words 'accoutred' and 'frowsty barn' almost match in terms of sound, but they come from quite different registers of discourse – the first sounding heraldic, armorial, to do with the past, the second summing up a casual modern judgement. This poem is about the difference between these two registers, and about the way the individual consciousness can be aware of this difference, but also, in the presence of the church and perhaps thus in the presence of God, span it.

font vessel for baptism
lectern desk from which the Bible is read
Irish sixpence Irish coinage is not accepted in the UK (though UK coinage, prior to the advent of the euro, was accepted in the Republic of Ireland), hence it is here symbolic of worthless money
pyx container for the communion wafer
dubious here means 'of dubious origin' and 'for dubious purposes'
simples herbal remedies
advised notice that this needs to be given three syllables

rood-lofts galleries over the screen at the entrance to the part of the church containing the altar

ruin-bibber Larkin's own term for somebody who samples ruins for their savour, like wine

randy ironically likens the taste for ruins to a taste for sex

gown-and-bands refers to clerical dress

myrrh perfume carried by one of the three wise men at the Nativity, redolent of death

accoutred decorated

frowsty fusty, musty

blent an archaic version of blended

MR BLEANEY (FROM THE WHITSUN WEDDINGS)

The narrator reconstructs the life and habits of the previous occupant of the room where he is lodging, and speculates on the meaning of that life and on what it might have felt like to live in such meagre circumstances

We have to picture as the **persona** of this poem a man who is looking for accommodation. In the opening stanza we hear his potential landlady describing to him the previous occupant of the room to let, Mr Bleaney. The room is unpleasant: cheap and not cared for. But the protagonist finds himself entering in his imagination into the life that Bleaney might have led here.

Clearly the landlady thought highly of him, and they got on all right together despite the lack of amenities in the room. The **protagonist** decides to rent the room, and finds himself increasingly involved with Bleaney, wondering about his life: he is forced to hear the wireless set which – he supposes – Bleaney persuaded the landlady to buy. He claims in the fifth stanza that he has come to know all about Bleaney, his leisure habits, his family.

But, as is so frequently the case with Larkin's poems, in the sixth stanza we find ourselves invited to an abrupt change of mood. The commonplaces of the first part of the poem become a springboard for a meditation on life and death, and specifically on the importance of the individual to the general course of the world. We are invited to wonder whether Bleaney – whoever he was – was contented with this bleak (the word is apposite) room; or whether he had glimpsed that even to live in such a room betrayed one's own worthlessness. If the latter is the case, then implicitly the poet, who is Bleaney's successor in this same room, is finding himself asking the same questions of himself; and are they questions about some particular temporary room, or about life envisaged *as* a bedsit?

Whatever it may mean literally, 'at the Bodies' means metaphorically 'in a body' and this introduces us to the notion that Bleaney's tenancy of the room is akin to our tenancy of the physical. The 'they' of 'They moved him' can thus be nothing but death.

The contrast between the chaos of the curtains which do not fit, the 'Tussocky' land outside, and the landlady's claim that Bleaney took care of her garden is stark: what does it mean to cultivate some small strip when all around is chaos, death and despair?

Notice that in the passages descriptive of the room Larkin omits the definite and the indefinite article: 'Bed, upright chair, sixty-watt bulb'. The effect of this is to generalise this room as a site for life, to claim that we might all end up in this kind of place, a place which is available all over the world.

'Fags' and 'saucer-souvenir' are redolent of a lower-class world. Larkin is certainly saying that Bleaney and his landlady belong to this world; whether he is also saying that he is himself of this world or whether he is saying that such a world permanently threatens him are questions on which we are left to speculate.

All through the fifth stanza there runs the parlance of the lower classes – it is not clear whether we are talking here about the working class or the lower-middle class – in the 'four aways', an **allusion** to the football pools; in Frinton and Stoke, notoriously unfashionable places.

The 'yearly frame', however, deliberately betrays the poet 'framing' this unremarkable life which he is ... reinventing? inventing? remembering? Perhaps we are here in the presence of the protagonist's own past, a past which he has tried to throw off through education, for example, but to which he finds himself in imagination perpetually returning.

The last stanzas stand in **syntactic** relation to the 'I know' of stanza four; for this is all that the protagonist does not 'know'. What he does not know is the level of Bleaney's self-awareness. What the poet sees is the waste, the triviality of Bleaney's life; what he does not know is whether Bleaney himself was aware of this. To the poet this room is redolent of death, as well it might be, since Bleaney's life effectively ended here. But did Bleaney himself appreciate the dreadful end to which life had brought him? Did he grin and shiver, like a skeleton, knowing that this final condition of his was the true measure of his worth? And if he did, does this imply that we too should understand that the insufficiency of our environment, the 'hired box' in which we perhaps live, is a true and just reward for our insufficiency as human beings?

tussocky unkempt
fags colloquial term for cigarettes
jabbering set a radio which, to the poet, makes no sense because he hears it only as background noise
hired box here means a rented room, but with connotations of a horse-box, and consequently of being manipulated without understanding where one is going

AN ARUNDEL TOMB (FROM THE WHITSUN WEDDINGS)

A meditation on the medieval tomb effigy of a couple, wondering about the relation between the art that has created the image, the actual life the couple might have lived, and the historical processes that have transformed the world since their time

This poem is unusual for Larkin. Although there are lyrical moments in many of his other poems, they are usually undercut by an all-pervading **irony**; but here the **lyrical** note, the celebration of past lives, is allowed to stand for itself.

We are looking at a medieval tomb; on that tomb lie the sculptured effigies of the 'earl and countess'. These effigies are weathered by the centuries such that their faces are 'blurred', but the observing eye, playing over this vagueness, lights upon the still vivid detail of their hands still clasped in each other's.

The poet enters a reverie, wondering whether this detail, which now appears to him so important, might have been of little significance when they commissioned – before their deaths – the anonymous sculptor to produce their monument. To them and to the sculptor perhaps this detail was merely a triviality compared with the perceived importance of preserving their names, their family's honour.

They would probably have imagined, the poet says in the fourth stanza, that it was their name which would carry continuing importance; instead, he suggests, it is this slight 'grace' of art which is now the only source of interest. The 'tenantry' has gone away; in other words the old feudal certainties on which the earl and countess no doubt based their lives, and also their hopes for remembrance after death, have now vanished, and all that remains of interest is the beauty of their posture: we care 'To look, not read'.

And so 'Time has transfigured them into / Untruth' – the meanings carried by their lives and deaths have been changed by the further passage of time. We do not know whether the earl and countess were or were not an especially faithful or admirable couple, but the accident by which time has failed to erode their clasped hands nonetheless means that we, the later generations, can still find in them an emblem for lasting love. At the same time we need to bear in mind that the reasons why this emblem persists are themselves at the mercy of time, as indeed is love itself.

> The stanza structure here is simple and almost architectural in its sturdiness, thereby exemplifying the persistence of the tomb. In itself it symbolises the strength by which art survives the erosion of time.

> The mention of the 'absurd' in the first stanza is a semi-evasion of the profundity of what he is saying (characteristic of Larkin); but the 'sharp tender shock' of the second stanza reverses the flow of this irony, reminding us that no matter how thick our skins may seem to be, we can still be touched and moved by the accidental.

> In the third stanza we encounter some of the many effects Larkin produces through **alliteration**: there are the 'f' sounds of 'faithfulness in effigy', and more obviously the sliding, continuing sounds of the 's' in 'sweet commissioned grace', which will later be echoed in 'supine stationary voyage'. All of this is a reminder of sleep, the soporific, yet thereby underlines the unconscious means by which survival occurs.

AN ARUNDEL TOMB

Notice that in the fifth stanza, where Larkin is beginning to talk about the centuries, the changes which have occurred between the lifetimes of the earl and countess and his own age, the stanza itself is broken up, like history perhaps, or like a ploughed field. The smoothness which has earlier in the poem replicated the smooth, sinuous lines of the prone effigies is now replaced by the broken, jagged shapes of verse lines which do not conform to sentence structure. In the very form of the verse Larkin is questioning this rigidity: are these feudal forms genuinely surviving, or do they lie in opposition to history? Do these effigies represent something we can still find operative in our daily lives, or are they a heritage which we have to break up, to overcome?

The 'endless altered people' (the pun on 'altar' is intended, because there are hints of an act of worship here) represent a different truth, but not necessarily a better one. The 'trough / Of smoke' reminds us of that supreme image of death and the glory of mortality, the seventeenth-century poet John Donne's 'bracelet of bright hair about the bone' (from 'The Relic').

What then are 'untruth' and 'fidelity'? Evidence, perhaps, that love is all-conquering but we can only half-believe this – perhaps because of the age in which we live, perhaps because we ourselves, as were the earl and countess, are proudly and humiliatingly mortal.

little dogs under their feet conventional tomb trappings of a knight
pre-baroque here refers to an artistic period before excessive embellishment, a time when clear lines, artistic, moral and social, could be picked out
unarmorial here, 'without real distinction' in all senses
skeins loosely tied lengths of thread
blazon coat-of-arms; here, evidence that they lived

COMMENTARIES — THE WHITSUN WEDDINGS

THE WHITSUN WEDDINGS (FROM THE WHITSUN WEDDINGS)

One of the best-known of all Larkin's poems. The protagonist is on a train and is awakened from a reverie by sounds of celebration. He realises that this is Whitsun, a traditional occasion for weddings, and this leads him into a series of meditations on the many courses life can take

Here the **protagonist** is on a train journey. The train is slow, the whole mood is unhurried, and Larkin brings alive for us the unremarkable sights one encounters on any provincial train journey.

He has not intended to travel at Whitsun; indeed, we realise that he has no association with Whitsun as a ceremony. Therefore in stanza three we learn that he is not looking out for evidence of the popularity – a time-honoured popularity – of Whitsun as an auspicious time for marriages.

As the train moves through station after station he begins to realise that the sounds he is hearing cannot simply be 'porters larking with the mails', and he notices at last that, on every station, there are families seeing bride and bridegroom off on their honeymoons.

In 'each face seemed to define / Just what it saw departing' the **persona** is brought face to face with the evidence of people trusting in new beginnings, but he cannot see it quite as that; instead, he sees marriage more as a continuation of the failings of the past, the 'uncle shouting smut' etc. He glimpses something significant here – 'Free at last' – but refers it back to the inescapability of convention with 'shuffling gouts of steam'.

In the final stanza, however, we are confronted by a crucial image which seems to cast doubt on the persona's smug refusal of change: in the image of arrows/rainshower it is as though Larkin is saying that although these weddings, these acts of trust, repeated in the face of the continual disillusionment offered by life might be considered as mere acts of conventional piety, he nonetheless recognises that he cannot know the outcome of them or is unable really to feel the oft-repeated hope they represent: who is to deny that somewhere, somehow, these hopes might be fulfilled?

> This poem demonstrates a problem in Larkin's poetry in general: what is the relation between the **ironic** and the non-ironic perception? For example, in the fourth stanza he portrays the families of the

newly-weds in highly unflattering terms. But whose is this perception? Is it Larkin's, or that of his persona? Does Larkin mean us to accept this as an unchallengeable portrayal of a certain class, or does he offer it to us as evidence of social prejudice?

He treads a thin line here, but saves himself by an unblemished accuracy of description. We can find it, for example, in the famous lines about London's 'squares of wheat': here Larkin reaches for an image which conjoins London as a place *seen* and as a place *imagined from maps* (as it would be to the wedding parties) and, superbly, finds it.

There are dozens of images in this poem which demonstrate that extraordinary mastery: 'a street / Of blinding windscreens', 'the reek of buttoned carriage-cloth', 'Bright knots of rail'. In all of them Larkin manages to conjoin a participatory perception with the observation of a stranger. He is both part of these scenes and aside from them. His persona, we might say, is fatally implicated in this world of perms and nylon gloves, yet is also ceaselessly aware of his distance from a society which, for all its gaucheness and grotesquerie, might yet be the only one which could save him from his isolation.

This poem is as much about the protagonist's isolation, his willed rejection of what he perceives, as it is about the Whitsun weddings themselves. The weddings stand as a double image: of that which one rejects on aesthetic grounds, and also as that which one envies because it provides evidence of a living, if debased, community.

'The Whitsun Weddings' is thus a poem emblematic of the ambiguity of community: does belonging to a community involve being a self which one does not want to be, or is it a reminder that one might be rescued from the isolation which is here **symbolised** by the solitary train journey, on which others may be seen only through impermeable windows?

Whitsun the seventh Sunday after Easter, also known as Pentecost, celebrated by Christians annually to commemorate the descent of the Holy Spirit to the apostles fifty days after Easter
carriage-cloth upholstery

COMMENTARIES   SELF'S THE MAN

skirls shrill cries
larking playing about
pomaded treated with hair oil
standing Pullmans railway coaches waiting in a siding

SELF'S THE MAN   (FROM THE WHITSUN WEDDINGS)

Larkin contrasts himself with a mythical other, Arnold, with a view to talking about who is the more selfish. Beneath this, what he is discussing is, as is customary with Larkin, the contrast between his own state of bachelorhood and the fate of the married man

The first stanza sets the tone of heavy **irony** that obtains throughout the poem. The poet claims that it might be argued that 'Arnold' is less selfish than himself, but immediately undermines this thought by suggesting that Arnold married his wife for reasons that had purely to do with his own comfort and fear of failure.

He then goes on – apparently – to detail Arnold's hen-pecked life, the difficulties he faces in having any time to call his own, the dire necessities under which he is put in order fully to acquit his role as a married man and, perhaps even more importantly, as a father – and, indeed, as a son-in-law. The poet concludes from this, in the fifth stanza, what any reasonable comparison of his life with Arnold's would immediately conclude: that he is the selfish one, and that Arnold's life – despite what has been said about his motivations in the first stanza – is a model of self-sacrifice.

The last three stanzas, however, begin by seeking to reverse this judgement. Arnold, it is suggested, ended up in this condition not through any magnanimity of his own but rather because he was 'out for his own ends'. This suggests to the poet that really there is not much in it, that he and Arnold have both been governed by self-interest, even if their perceptions as to how that self-interest might be maximised have been radically different.

The last stanza, however, again marks a break in the apparent direction of the poem by focusing attention back on the poet himself, although the question of where the poem ends up in terms of the different varieties of selfishness on display remains to some extent an open one.

Certainly in its opening phases, what stands out most about this poem is the crudity of its language – the entirety of the second stanza would be an example. This raises an important question which could be applied to much of Larkin's poetry: does his use of particularly imprecise registers taken from everyday speech render his own poetry similarly imprecise, or does some curious transmutation happen through the medium itself? The phrase 'the kiddies' clobber' would in any other context appear merely stupid or banal, the product of the verbally challenged; what happens to such phrases when they appear in Larkin's poems?

There is a similar sense of **bathos** in some of the rhymes – 'houses' and 'trousers', for example – which we may think succeed in context, but which seem highly unlikely to thrive *outside* that context without calling down a certain derision. But then, perhaps 'derision' is one of the most useful words to apply to this poem: the poet's derision of Arnold, certainly, but also perhaps the poet's derision of himself for imagining himself fundamentally different from Arnold in the way he has structured his life.

The conclusion of the poem is puzzling. After asserting that Arnold is less selfish than himself, and then appearing to reverse or at least to neutralise this verdict by pointing out that both Arnold and he have responded to similar intentions (even if – and this is crucial to Larkin's poetry in general – those intentions have not been understood by either man at the time), he now seems to mount an entirely different regime of argument. Larkin asserts that he is 'a better hand' that he has a superior strategy in playing the 'game' of life.

What hovers most disconcertingly over this final stanza, however, is the spectre of the 'van'. In this van we sense Larkin's continuing preoccupation with ambulances and similar vehicles sent to convey people away – on medical grounds by an ambulance, on grounds of sanity by some more mysterious 'van', or on the final grounds of death, where the hearse performs all these functions of sequestration in a single, final, fatal act.

The claims which have seemed throughout the poem to be potentially true of humanity at large are radically reduced by this final stanza. Instead of speaking of two different kinds of life a man might lead, Larkin suddenly reveals to us that he is – at least by this point in the poem – simply speaking of what he as an individual might be able to 'stand'; and even here, of course, the last line further undercuts any of the claims to universality or certainty the poem might previously have appeared to be making.

clobber slang for 'clothes', or 'belongings' in general
drier could be clothes-drier or, less expensively, a hairdryer
nippers toddlers, small children

HOME IS SO SAD (FROM THE WHITSUN WEDDINGS)

A poem of intense regret: regret for life's failed opportunities, regret for the past which remains unfulfilled and cannot be regained

There is no real complexity to the content of this poem. The poet pictures 'home': he pictures it as empty, 'bereft', no longer having the 'heart' to continue. He then turns to the past – or rather, perhaps, to the remaining traces of the past – in order to contrast the forlorn condition of the present with the largely occluded memory of ambitious and optimistic beginnings – beginnings, perhaps, of a marriage or a relationship.

The ways in which the theme is worked out in the poem show Larkin at his finest, as is quite frequently the case when he is, as it were, working in miniature. The vocabulary is plain, stark, quite largely monosyllabic. The rhymes are simple. There is little or no attempt at vivid or detailed description – the only two outstanding adjectives in the poem are 'sad' and 'joyous', which are the principal points of contrast in the poem – but even those are not imagistically precise, they do not directly help to conjure a picture for us.

And yet a picture *is* conjured here, in the most remarkable of ways and by the most minute of strokes. For example, the second line – 'Shaped to the comfort of the last to go' – appears to be a kind of transferred **epithet**: although it seems to refer to the house, the image it actually produces has much more to do with a chair or sofa, thus reinforcing the vividness of the idea of somebody having just left the scene.

In a way, the lack of description seems to render the poem more powerful, perhaps because it allows the reader to fit his or her own 'shape' into the vacant spaces of the poem and the 'home' alike. Consider, for example, the difference between 'it withers so', and the effect that would have been produced had the word 'so' been omitted. On the one hand, the word 'so' suggests something limitless; only the reader can supply a specific sense of just how far things have 'withered', the poem does not short-circuit this specificity, this challenge to the reader's own memories. On the other hand, there is something forlorn and hopeless about the word 'so' itself in this context, as though it signifies that there is no point in even attempting to measure the appalling distance between hope and fulfilment.

The 'shot' that has 'Long fallen wide' necessarily reminds us of those other arrows in the last lines of 'The Whitsun Weddings', and one could almost read 'Home is so Sad' as a deadly coda to the hopes expressed – even if in severely circumscribed form – in the title poem 'The Whitsun Weddings'. After all the hopes, the bright morning, all that is left is an empty house. The 'You' of the eighth line is crucial: it is at once entirely personal and specific, it addresses the reader directly, implicating him/her in the scenario of the poem; and completely general, as though in experiencing this sense of loss and disappointment we are merely participating in the inevitable defeat of hope which is the universal human lot.

The sense of being personally addressed is intensified towards the close of the poem, as we are specifically enjoined to 'Look at the pictures and the cutlery'. This is not, we notice, any particular kinds of picture or cutlery but rather the ordinary, undistinguished paraphernalia by which – according to the poet – we are all surrounded, but which has ceased to carry or be enlivened by the meaning – of love, or of warmth – that once it bore.

The extraordinary ending 'That vase' immediately brings us up as close as it is possible to get to the objects within the poem. As readers, we have to do a double-take; it is as if the poet is asserting that you, or I, actually *know* this house, it is no longer a generalised home but rather our own place, a place that we have vacated but which still holds memories – memories betrayed by our own absence from the scene. We could say that what the poem ends with is a terrible, and terrifying, shock of recognition which leaves us ineluctably implicated in the melancholy which frames it.

FAITH HEALING   (FROM THE WHITSUN WEDDINGS)

A meditation on the question of what it is that makes life worth living, and the lengths to which people are willing to go to persuade themselves that they are capable of experiencing love. Is it necessary to believe in possibilities even though we might feel that those possibilities are the product of charlatanry?

The scene is a meeting presided over by a visiting American faith healer. The crowd is very large and the so-called healer has little time to speak to any individual. The effect on the people in the audience is enormous and varied. Some leave; but some are unable to, because their experience with the faith healer – whether he has genuine gifts or not – has stirred up such depths within them. They find themselves projecting on to him all the thwarted wishes of their past lives; despite themselves they find themselves believing that he has a message for each individual.

In the third stanza the sense of this disturbance increases as Larkin suggests to us how many people suffer from not being loved enough; so fiercely do they feel this lack that they are willing to fill it with any experience, no matter how sham it may be. The last lines point up the ways in which, in everyday life, people keep themselves braced and defended against disappointment; what happens with the faith healer is that they are allowed to relax these defences, thawing into the long withheld tears. Yet the final phrase, 'all time has disproved', ends the poem on a characteristically pessimistic note, for if time has indeed disproved the possibility of real love, then what can a mere faith healer do about it?

> The crucial opposition in the poem is between the mechanical and suspect nature of the faith healer's ministrations and the stark reality of the emotions which are released in his presence. In the first stanza this is pointed up in the description of the healer's 'warm spring rain of loving care', the image of the spring rain also introduces us to the idea of people 'thawing', the ending, if only temporary, of a long icy winter which is Larkin's image for the way in which people are

encouraged by the presence of the faith healer to relax their automatic defences.

In the second stanza the attitude of the narrator to the crowd becomes complicated. There is deep sympathy in the view of these people 'twitching and loud / With deep hoarse tears', people who are still waiting 'To re-awake at kindness', but what do we feel when we read that 'Their thick tongues blort, their eyes squeeze grief'? Here we seem to be in the presence of people who are almost reduced to a debased, animal-like state: 'sheepishly stray', 'dumb'. Behind this emotional complexity, we can sense a problem which Larkin is trying to explore: on the one hand there is a wish to be among these people, to be able to feel the moment of release, while on the other there is a conventional embarrassment at seeing people 'letting go' of themselves.

At the beginning of the third stanza it seems that a mood of scorn has taken over: 'Moustached in flowered frocks they shake'. But after that the poem grows increasingly **lyrical** as Larkin stands back from the scene and offers us a meditation on love and lovelessness. We are not asked to judge whether the feelings portrayed are accurate, i.e. whether these individuals really have been loved or not. What we are asked to recognise is that in all of us there survives a child who feels cheated of all the love that might have been his or hers, and it is this hidden child within who reawakes at the touch of the faith healer.

Is the faith healer genuine? We have no means of knowing. The **persona** seems to suggest he is not ('Their heads are clasped abruptly'); but then as the poem develops we see that the persona is himself not entirely to be trusted, he displays a certain envy of the situation. In the end it does not matter: as has been emphasised from the beginning, it is the voice of the faith healer that matters, the fact that he can say 'dear child' and *sound* sincere. **Metaphorically**, Larkin underlines that this is the depths ('deep American voice') speaking to the depths ('deep hoarse tears') and thus communicating at levels where our reason counts for nothing.

blort Larkin's own word, to suggest 'blurting out', clumsiness, lack of control

TALKING IN BED   (FROM THE WHITSUN WEDDINGS)

A poem which expresses misgivings about the possibility of human intimacy, and thus touches upon the problematic value of human communication in general

Larkin takes a situation – talking in bed – which is conventionally supposed to be 'easiest', in the sense of easy to do and also of being a product of being 'at one's ease'. But this 'emblem of two people being honest', this image of a conversation within which there are no barriers to sincerity, he claims, is never fully lived up to; as time goes by, within a relationship or a marriage, then a certain silence encroaches, a certain reserve or perhaps a drought of things to say.

The presence of two people in this situation ought, perhaps, to represent a 'unique distance from isolation', the solution to loneliness; but instead words dry up, and even the potential for kindness and truth becomes degraded into a system of evasions, a way of finding ways of *not* saying words that might be damaging or indeed devastating in their consequence.

This is a cruelly pessimistic poem, although, as often with Larkin, the cruelty seems to be applied at least as much to the **protagonist**'s incapacities as to those of anybody else. The word 'emblem' in the first stanza hints that this is a poem about the failure of ideals, the apparently inevitable destruction of the **symbolic** and the beautiful as they are worn away, by the winds of the ordinary, by the forces of banality and repetition.

The poem falls into three parts. After the first four lines, which seem to express more wistful regret than hope, there comes a second part which conjures a linked set of **images**. These images are looming, threatening, menacing; they show the uncomprehending nature of the outside world, its chronic indifference towards the petty arrangements of human intimacy. Whatever is happening out there – the 'unrest' of the wind, the dispersal of clouds, the 'heaping up' of the outer world of urban materiality – it cares nothing for us. Either this uncaringness infects human relationships with a kind of hopelessness, or feelings of hopelessness in human relationships combine to produce a sense of an uncaring outer world.

Either way, it makes no difference: in the end, Larkin says, language and communication grind down towards an unavoidable silence, and to a situation where our feelings of dislike or boredom towards the other – or perhaps simply of boredom with ourselves – form a kind of constant undertow. Communication, then, even the most supposedly intimate of communications, does not form an exchange of honest feeling, rather a method of concealment, a way of hiding from the other the dearth, the depthlessness of our feelings. There is, perhaps, a little salvation to be found in the closing line – as there remains a concern not to be 'untrue' or 'unkind' – but certainly not much.

TAKE ONE HOME FOR THE KIDDIES   (FROM THE WHITSUN WEDDINGS)

About pets and their significance, in terms of love, possession and the experience of death

On the surface, this is a poem about pets. Rabbits, hamsters, or whatever they are, we see them in the pet-shop window, far away from any kind of natural habitat and exposed to the stare of every passer-by. Naturally, children are attracted to them and persuade their mothers to buy them but, as we see in the second stanza, the novelty soon wears off and the pets die.

Under the surface, this is a highly complex poem, although this complexity is masked brilliantly by simplicity of language and **syntax**. Note, incidentally, a line characteristic of Larkin, 'Huddled by empty bowls, they sleep', which is syntactically and rhythmically identical to a crucial part of 'Faith Healing', 'Moustached in flowered frocks they shake'.

Although we are sure it is pets that Larkin is talking about, he never says so directly, and in the first stanza this allows us to think more generally about others who may be 'Huddled by empty bowls', human victims of poverty and exploitation. The child's vision of this is direct but also thoughtlessly cruel: to the child these pets appear as mere possessions. There is a crucial ambiguity in the final word of the first stanza, 'keep': it has an ordinary, literal sense of owning a pet, but it also suggests the staving off of death. Either the pet itself will never die, or we somehow use pets as a reinforcement against our own deaths.

The second stanza is linguistically controlled by the extraordinary rhyming of 'novel' and 'shovel': the rapid, rather offhand sounds of these words, combined with the fact that to rhyme them at all suggests a certain sloppiness, both contribute to the offhand way in which Larkin is deliberately dealing with death in this stanza. There is nothing here of tragedy or grief, no real emotional intensity, no real perception of other creatures. There is not even a wish to explore the realities of death, and this is why Larkin uses the word 'somehow', to suggest the unexamined way in which people handle even matters of ultimate seriousness.

For the children, the death of their pet is just another game, indicated by the last line. But if Larkin is likening these children to people at large, with their possessiveness and lack of thought and fellow-feeling, then the poem turns into a savage indictment of the limited level on which we all live – a poem about heartlessness and the absence of moral and emotional distinction.

Notice the careful patterning of sounds: the **alliterations** in the first line ('shallow' and 'shadeless') and in the third ('No dark, no dam') are designed to reinforce our sense of the inescapability of the pets' situation. But this alliteration returns with redoubled force towards the end with the repetition of 'fetch' and the double 'sh' sound of 'shoebox' and 'shovel'. This reminds us that what is really repetitive, really inevitable, no matter what games we try to play with it, is death.

dam beavers make dams; also means 'mother'

A STUDY OF READING HABITS   (FROM THE WHITSUN WEDDINGS)

A heavily ironic poem about the value, or valuelessness, of reading, and thus about the value of literature itself. It seems to derogate the whole question of reading and writing, culminating in the celebrated line, perhaps surprising from a poet, 'Books are a load of crap'

The first stanza, from the beginning, raises confusing and complicated questions about the purpose and nature of reading, especially for the young. The protagonist appears to have enjoyed reading, although he refers to it in characteristically demeaning terms ('getting my nose in a book'), but is unwilling entirely to own up to this unfashionable preoccupation by wearing glasses. What is uncertain is whether his capacity to fight 'dirty dogs twice my size' represents a real – if surprising – aptitude, or whether it has more to do with his wishful transference of his identification with literary characters onto the real circumstances of his life.

At any rate, when he is forced to wear glasses (betraying, we may presume, the bookishness of which he is at least half ashamed) he retreats further into fantasy – identifying with vampires, with sexually predatory heroes. All this, however, so the protagonist claims, belongs to the past; he has now largely given up books because they have come to seem too familiar, too formulaic, and because they do not represent the real brutality of the world. He has learned a kind of lesson, but it is really an anti-lesson, which is that books do not constitute a true preparation for 'real life' – whatever that may be.

> It is important to notice the slang register in which much of this poem is written: 'getting my nose in a book'; 'keep cool', 'the old right hook', 'dirty dogs', just to take up the references from the first stanza. With the use of this language, the protagonist already identifies himself with those who despise and disparage books, while at the same time demonstrating how far he has himself identified with certain types of 'genre fiction', where the apparently weak and feeble hero triumphs against all odds.

> This slang discourse returns in the second stanza – 'just my lark', 'ripping times' – but now, perhaps, with a darker undertow. There is a hint here of violence, of menace, which the reader might justly suspect to have less to do with the books themselves than with the protagonist's fears, his need to use his reading to counteract his anxieties about everyday life.

> Notice, at the beginning of the third stanza, the omission of the initial 'I' before 'Don't read much now': the reduction of language to a kind of telegraphic style, evidencing the failure of what one might consider to be a proper or correct use of words. The two **images** here, of the 'dude' who 'lets the girl down' and 'the chap / Who's yellow',

COMMENTARIES   THE LARGE COOL STORE

although they are in one sense taken from cheap fiction (and it is as cheap fiction that the poet is representing the entire world of books) both also seem to represent the 'hero' himself: he has come to see that his role in the world is not heroic but rather as a bit-part player, as unreliable, as a coward. It is, we may surmise, for this reason – because he has come to see the painful impossibility of living up to or within the fantasy ideals proffered by fiction – that he resorts to the destructiveness, the scorn and contempt, of the final phrases.

the old right hook a term for a specific – and specifically 'terminal' – punch in boxing
dirty dogs a **parodic** version of a conventional way of referring to the villains in popular literature
specs short for spectacles
lark game, pastime, hobby – something done for fun and without involvement or feeling
ripping a pun on 'ripping yarns', a term frequently used to describe and to advertise boys' adventure stories, and 'ripping' in the sense of tearing or gouging, the attributes of the vampire
yellow cowardly – but perhaps also a racial stereotype of the oriental or specifically the Chinese when represented (as so often) as villains in 'western fiction'.
Get stewed a slang insult

THE LARGE COOL STORE   (FROM THE WHITSUN WEDDINGS)

Through the imagery of a shop, this poem contrasts an everyday world of work with the fantasies that might occupy the night-time. Whether the version of night-time proffered by a commercialised world represents any real alternative remains uncertain

We are to picture a large shop selling clothing – quite a cheap shop, one where there is something for everybody to afford. The poet's eye strays over some of these clothes, and he thinks about the working people who are likely to wear them. But then his eye jumps to the 'Modes For Night', the stands of ladies' nightdresses. He sees these garments, their shapes and colours, and he senses a kind of misfit between the daylight world of

39

factories and workaday clothes and this night-time world. Can these two worlds really be shared?

As he meditates on the problem, his mind turns over a number of solutions. It may be that at night we do move into a different world, that these 'Baby-Dolls and Shorties' are the nearest we can get to a contemporary representation of the 'differentness' of love. Or it may be that the difference is really one between men and women; that the sober 'browns and greys' belong to a world of men's work, whereas the 'Lemon, sapphire, moss-green, rose' are women's colours. Or it may be that these nightdresses represent only a fantasy about women – and if so, that fantasy is not altogether a pleasant or coherent one since it requires women to be ever 'new', fresh and clean, and yet 'synthetic', since the materials he is describing are man-made (perhaps in both senses of the term). It requires of women that they represent ecstasy, passion, in an almost pornographic way, while at the same time being 'natureless', unnaturally clothed and unnatural in themselves.

> This is a difficult poem because it depends on a number of words which are quite specific to the time of its composition. Yet this very fact reminds us of one of the poem's themes, which is that these clothes are synthetic, throwaway, merely the stuff of a day's fashion.
>
> At the beginning we sense no animosity on the poet's part; it is obviously good that there are cheap clothes available, that they are displayed 'plainly' so that the purchaser can see the goods on offer and make sensible choices. Nevertheless, even here we wonder whether Larkin is also commenting on the poverty of lives led in 'low terraced houses', low in literal shape but also in the social order.
>
> It is when the poet observes the 'Modes For Night' that the tone becomes more critical. The word 'mode' is a pseudo-sophisticated word, meant to persuade us that these cheap clothes are like their high-fashion equivalents, when we know that they are 'Machine-embroidered', cheaply made, mass produced. They are thin and not made to last, so that we will always need to buy more. We also need to keep buying these clothes because they will rapidly go out of fashion; in this way they are designed to increase our consumption. The colours Larkin uses are carefully chosen: 'lemon' is an obviously

synthetic colour, as is 'rose'; 'sapphire' probably just means some garish shade of blue, but renamed to make it seem more attractive. 'Moss-green' reminds us sharply of the natural world, but only to contrast it with these 'unnatural' colours. The materials ('Bri-Nylon') are also unnatural, as are the shapes, which are chosen artificially to exaggerate the female form. As they 'Flounce in clusters', they seem to have a life of their own.

We move, halfway through the third stanza, into a characteristic meditation on what these clothes mean about our relationships, our attitudes to each other. The 'They' of line 14 are the nightdresses; 'that world' is the other world, the grimy, darkened world of factories and terraced housing.

The three hypotheses Larkin offers us at the end are in descending order of pleasantness. He suggests to begin with that perhaps, even in a debased form, these clothes have to do with love, even with quite powerful emotions ('separate and unearthly'); for a moment, the poem flickers on the edge of romanticism. His next suggestion (which can be rearranged to read 'how separate and unearthly women are') is less acceptable, for it clearly relegates women to a different realm, as though there is an unbridgeable gap between the sexes. The third hypothesis, which is the one with which we are left, is less acceptable still since it suggests that these clothes embody only an infantile fantasy of women which does violence to their reality.

The poem is held together by a complex rhyme scheme. Each stanza rhymes ABABA, but the A lines in stanzas one and three also rhyme together (from 'clothes' down to 'shows'), as do the A lines in stanzas two and four, although in this case it is a half-rhyme (from 'houses' down to 'ecstasies'). The other tremendous skill Larkin shows here is of taking words from a common, throwaway vocabulary and using them to suggest an argument of depth and emotional strength.

Knitwear the term under which such a store would display jumpers, cardigans and the like
Summer Casuals would include trousers and skirts of light material

THE LARGE COOL STORE

Hose socks, tights: like 'Modes', the word is a deliberately inflated one to persuade us of a spurious quality
Bri-Nylon a cheap, popular synthetic material
Baby-Dolls and Shorties revealing nightwear for women

Nothing to be said   (from The Whitsun Weddings)

Like others of Larkin's poems, about the passing of a way of life – not here a particular way of life but rather the general passage of time within which things change as they move slowly down towards death

The first stanza traces this passage across a variety of cultural situations. The 'nations vague as weed', we may suppose, are vague partly because they are largely unknown or forgotten. However, these figures from the remote past or perhaps from the geographically distant – the 'nomads' and 'tribes' – suffer no more than the families in contemporary western mill-towns, whose established way of life is passing away with equally unavoidable certainty.

What has been important for these people, groups, cultures, as the poet sees it – or perhaps what is important to him as he thinks about them – is precisely their difference one from other, their 'separate ways'. It is not necessarily that one is better than another, but rather that difference itself is to be prized whether it be in the uncultivated surroundings of a pig-hunt or in the comparatively cultured ones of a garden party.

Yet this thought of difference rapidly disappears in the third stanza: what is obliterating it is not, in the poet's view, some inexorable political or social process – technology or globalisation, for example – but rather the way in which everything becomes equal in the dark light of death. If you tell people that, he concludes, to some it 'Means nothing'; for others it may instead leave 'Nothing to be said'.

> The phrase which concludes the first stanza, 'Life is slow dying', is curious in several ways. It is rhythmically odd – one would more naturally expect 'slowly' instead of 'slow'. The phrase as given us is also remarkably poised. On the surface one might assimilate it to the reading it would have if 'slow' were indeed merely a substitute for 'slowly', in other words as a pure mourning of the passing of ways of

life. However, to focus on the 'slow dying' is to reveal two further levels of potential meaning: the first, an optimistic one, might imply that it is indeed very hard to extinguish life, that there is something in life which resists death; the second, which undercuts this, is the reading that suggests that, therefore, life *is* 'slow dying', that all of life is inevitably tainted by the prospect of its ending.

The middle of the poem is structured around a series of oppositional pairs – 'building' and 'benediction'; 'love' and 'money'; the pig-hunt and the garden party; giving 'evidence' or 'birth'. All of these are put forward as examples of the multifariousness of human life, and thus are intended to intensify our mourning at the extinction with which they – and we – are inevitably faced.

The final phrase is similarly capable of more than one interpretation. One reading would suppose that the thought of death leaves 'Nothing to be said' in the sense that it totally summarises experience; there is indeed nothing else to say. Another reading, though, would have it that to hear the truth of the advance of death leaves nothing to be said because the hearer is so horrified by the revelation of death that all speech, and all purpose for speech, is stopped. The third, more **symbolic** reading would be that the hearer's life is itself stopped by hearing the thought of death; to hear that thought accurately and fully is, in fact, to die.

nomads people who live in no fixed place
cobble-close Larkin's own formulation, meaning 'as closely packed as cobbles on a road or path'
benediction blessing, implying ways of religious observance in general

WILD OATS   (FROM THE WHITSUN WEDDINGS)

This rueful and apparently slight poem shows Larkin at his most ironically self-deprecating; whether the tone is playful or tragic is largely a matter for the reader to decide

The memory with which the poem starts is vague and the tone is laconic, imprecise, very much the voice of a man telling an anecdote to friends –

'came in where I worked'. The scenario is simple: two girls come in, one of them clearly attractive to the narrator, the other not particularly so, although he does at least say that he can talk to her.

An affair develops with the second girl, and indeed the duration of the relationship – 'seven years' and 'over four hundred letters' – may perhaps seem somewhat startling after its meagrely and casually related beginnings. During this time, it seems, the **narrator** only encountered the 'English rose' twice, and felt – although he does suggest that his feelings might be unreliable – that she was laughing at him – or perhaps, indeed, at the two of them and at their unglamorous relationship.

The third stanza tells us that the break-up of the relationship was messy: 'after about five / Rehearsals'. The fact that the narrator says he learned a lesson about himself during the course of it is considerably undermined by the flippancy of 'Well, useful to get that learnt'. Whether the concluding reflection on the photos of the 'bosomy rose' adds any seriousness to the poem's moral, or rather emphasises the way in which the narrator has *not* learnt anything from these events, remains in doubt.

> As well as being a reflection on the narrator's own past, the poem does also have something to say about what one might term the 'cultural past' and consequently about the generational changes Larkin has seen and which form the basis of so many of his other better-known poems. We are initially alerted to this by the phrase 'in those days'; there is a clear implication that whatever the manners and mores were that controlled relationships between men and women 'twenty years ago', they have now changed – although, as we know from elsewhere in Larkin's corpus, supposedly too late for him.

> 'The whole shooting-match' is also, perhaps, a somewhat **archaic** turn of speech, and certainly not a very precise one: Larkin means to refer to the entire conduct of relationships, but by using this term he simultaneously places himself **ironically** in opposition to these norms and conventions, taking up his familiar position as the outsider.

> Not merely an outsider, however: the savagery with which Larkin sometimes treats his own persona in his poems comes out more pointedly in the second stanza, with the reference to the 'ten-guinea ring / I got back in the end'. There are, admittedly, two possible ways

of reading these lines. It is conceivable that he 'got' the ring back in the sense that it was sent back to him by his disappointed girl-friend; but it seems far more probable that the narrator has meanly cajoled the girl into returning the ring, even though doing so took some effort and presumably helped to ensure a dismal end to the relationship.

The phrase 'Unknown to the clergy' in the second stanza is also of interest. It may conceivably refer us back to Thomas Hardy's poem 'In a Cathedral City', a far more brilliantly melancholy poem about the loss of the object of love, but it also conjures up the phrase 'Without benefit of clergy', a phrase used to describe a sexual relationship outside wedlock. Of course, whether the relationship here being described was sexual or not is undefined in the poem; nevertheless, the sense of something furtive and illicit remains hovering within the stanza.

The third stanza is complex in tone. For the narrator to realise that he was 'too selfish, withdrawn, / And easily bored to love' seems at first glance a humble recognition of his own failings. There is, in fact, something of an ambiguity in the structure of the lines – do they imply that the narrator is unable to love, or unable to be loved? – but whichever way we read them there does seem to be a possibility that some genuine moral or emotional learning has gone on. But the fifth line completely deflates this; indeed, it makes even such a phrase as 'genuine moral or emotional learning' seem unbearably pretentious, for we are not meant to end up supposing that change has happened. On the contrary, the strongest possibility must be that for this character, change is not possible.

The ambiguities of the final three lines are manifold. One could say that again this is a poem about desire: it says that our desires may be pointed in certain directions, but these directions are permanently incapable of achievement, and, worse than that, they render the rest of our pursuits and ambitions pointless and trivial. The affair has, we might say, been unconsciously blighted by the very existence of 'beautiful' – or, we might say, by the unattainable existence of beauty itself. The 'fur gloves' are an obvious sexual **symbol**, but this hint of something more voluptuous is immediately suppressed and voided of any positive connotation by the narrator's denigration of the photographs (or, of course, possibly the gloves) as 'Unlucky charms'. If they are unlucky charms, then the world is ruled by fate and chance; and this gives the narrator a perfect excuse for his own behaviour and for his past – and, we expect, present – failures.

English rose the embodiment of a specifically English idea of beauty
specs short for spectacles

Essential Beauty   (FROM THE WHITSUN WEDDINGS)

The unreal world of advertising is sharply contrasted with the unpleasant facts of sickness and mortality which it seeks to conceal

The first stanza of this startling poem depends for its effect on the reader gradually realising that Larkin is talking about advertising boards. There are advertisements for bread, for custard, for motor-oil, for salmon; what they share is their complete inappropriateness to their surroundings ('Screen graves with custard').

What the advertisements present is a composite view of how life should be: 'golden butter', 'Well-balanced families', 'fine / Midsummer weather'. These pictures of healthy outdoor life are balanced by an idealised picture of the home: 'cups at bedtime', 'slippers on warm mats'.

But at the break between the two stanzas Larkin states baldly that these images have little or nothing to do with the realities of life. They relate to the real only as 'pure crust, pure foam'; in the real world nothing can live up to these images of purity, and thus advertisements create and thrive on dissatisfaction and social envy. In the advertisements pubs are 'dark raftered' taverns where the elegant disport themselves; in reality drink causes distress and poverty, just as advertisements for cigarettes really cause people to die.

As they die, they have a vision: a vision of 'essential beauty'. They have been led to think that this beauty could be brought into their lives by obeying the injunctions of the advertisements; but in the end all we are shown is that this vision of beauty will always elude us in the very moment that we think we can reach out and grasp it.

The very first line conjures up a vital image: the advertisements 'face all ways' not only in the literal sense but also in that they capture us at every point; there is no way we can escape their fantasised reflections and distortions of our desires. Thus the 'ends of streets' which are blocked are again not only literal but also the natural avenues of development which are 'blocked' by the lies told by advertisements.

The word 'groves' at the end of the fifth line is supposed to remind us of the sacred groves of ancient religions: advertising covers its objects with a sacred aura, but really there is nothing behind this apparent mystery – it is hollow and cruel. The rhyming of 'gutter' and 'butter' is an apt summary of the principal contrast Larkin is drawing. These two worlds, he is saying, can be held together only if we believe in a kind of magic, the magic represented in the 'groves' and also in the gesture of the 'small cube', as if this cube, which is no doubt made of gravy powder, could somehow supply the key to another, better world.

The word 'aligned' in line 13 suggests how neatly ordered the world of advertising is, how it seems able to repel all disturbance and threat; in the advertisements even the cats are neatly 'quarter-profile' (and here, of course, Larkin is also using our own knowledge of the way in which cats actually do often seem to arrange themselves in the most prepossessing way!).

The opposition which Larkin draws at the end of the first and beginning of the second stanzas is summarised in the words 'Reflect' and 'dominate'. These advertisements do not 'reflect', do not provide a recognisable image of the 'rained-on streets and squares'; rather, they display a world where the rain never falls, and thus provide images which seem more attractive than, and thus 'dominate', the outdoor world.

In the first part of the second stanza there are gentle hints that Larkin is mocking a Platonic view of the world. The Greek philosopher Plato claimed that the world which we see is purely insubstantial; to attain to wisdom and beauty we have to see through it to the 'essential' reality of things. Larkin is **parodying** this view in

ESSENTIAL BEAUTY — COMMENTARIES

saying that the apparent reality of advertisements dissolves as we approach: their claim to represent a real vision is purely illusory.

The final image is one of Larkin's finest. In it he manages to combine the everyday **pathos** of dying of lung cancer with a more universal image of the obscure object of desire. The image of 'that unfocused she' is not specific; it is, as Larkin uses it, a summation of all the hopes and dreams which we have, those hopes and dreams which are exploited by advertising. The word 'recognising' in the last line has a multitude of implications: according to the **syntactic** structure, it is the 'unfocused she' who recognises the observer in the moment of his death, but clearly this meaning can also be reversed. The very fact that it can be reversed raises further doubts which move beyond the poem and which Larkin does nothing to allay: doubts about whether this object of desire really exists outside ourselves, or whether what we are really shown in advertising is a distorted image of our own self.

cuts choice pieces
radiant bars an image for gas or electric fires
halfpenny half an old penny, approximately equivalent to one-sixth of a new penny
drag slang for 'a pull on a cigarette'

Sunny Prestatyn (FROM THE WHITSUN WEDDINGS)

Contrasts the apparently ideal worlds portrayed in advertising with the implicit deprivation that causes people to damage and deface objects of beauty

The poem centres on a poster advertising holidays in Prestatyn, a seaside resort in North Wales. The poster presents an entirely idealised view of the resort, including a 'Hotel with palms', but mainly it presents its audience with an image of a pretty girl, kneeling on the beach and laughing, in a posture of some abandon that inevitably trades on sexualised imagery.

The poster, we are told, was put up in March – a month which, symbolically, represents a far end of the year from the summer setting of the poster itself. But within a few weeks the poster has been defaced. Teeth and eyes have been disfigured; the sexual features of the girl's body have been grotesquely enlarged; and finally she has been set 'fairly astride' a set of male genitalia.

In the third stanza the poster decays further and acquires a knife mark before being actually partly torn off the billboard – whether by human action or through age the poem does not say. Like every poster, it is then replaced, but of course by something entirely different, in this case a poster for a campaign against cancer.

> The poem is neatly poised. On the one hand, we are brought to see that an image of beauty, if it is displayed in unprotected circumstances, will soon become the prey of people for whom such beauty is intolerable, either because of their own circumstances or because of a more or less uncontrollable destructiveness that may be a consequence of deprivation or may be a universal feature of humanity. But on the other, we might fairly feel uncomfortable with this reading. After all, the poster is not really an image of beauty, at least not in any obvious artistic sense. It is mass-produced, probably crudely depicted, exploitative in its use of sexual suggestiveness, and bears little or no relation to the actualities of Prestatyn.
>
> The advertisement itself, therefore, is a tissue of delusions; palm trees rarely thrive on the North Welsh coast, and the posture of the girl – with the emphasis on her thighs and her 'breast-lifting' arms – may well seem to invite the graffiti that come to disfigure her, as a sarcastic rejoinder to the lies on which the poster trades. The poet seems to feel both of these things. The phrase 'slapped up' at the beginning of the second stanza, although literally referring to the careless and unthought way in which the poster was put on the billboard, carries connotations of 'knocked up', a slang term for 'becoming pregnant', and these connotations seem to accuse the girl herself of the kind of sexual exploitation of which the makers of the poster are no doubt guilty.
>
> The graffiti are, of course, no more artistic – presumably less so – than the poster itself – they are merely 'scrawls', and what they depict is not depicted for pleasure but rather as a kind of scorn or contempt. In the third stanza, things take a turn for the more violent as we

learn first of the knife mark on the girl's mouth and then of the great tear through the poster.

This barely-suppressed violence, the poem appears to say, is endemic to our society. How, though, might this thought relate to the final image of the poem, the replacement of the Prestatyn poster by one saying *'Fight Cancer'*? There are, perhaps, several ways. We might take the term 'cancer' precisely to indicate the kind of venomous or offhand contempt that has clearly inspired the defacers of the first poster; we might see this as a social cancer, and thus conclude from the poem that a clear ethical point is being made. But a different reading would be far less positive, and would suggest that the world of advertising is so meaningless, so fraught with lies and fantasies, that even the apparently clear message *'Fight Cancer'* is downgraded by association, and thus, by implication, all discourse suffers from the draining of meaning characteristic of the Prestatyn poster.

hunk literally here means a 'piece' of coastline, but the slang term 'hunk' for a well-muscled and desirable young man seems to resonate with the rest of the poem

snaggle-toothed with uneven and crossed teeth, here the work of whoever has been drawing on the poster

boss-eyed squinting

tuberous similar to a tuber, here implying grotesquely large and ill-formed

Dockery and Son (FROM THE WHITSUN WEDDINGS)

The protagonist explores, in the context of a visit to his old college, questions about how decisions are made – or even whether we make decisions in our lives at all, rather than simply reacting to circumstances or having our choices dictated by unexamined assumptions and prejudices

In this well-known poem the **protagonist** returns to his old college, and finds himself involved in a conversation about a person called Dockery who was at the college at the same time. He is told that Dockery's son is now a student there.

He meditates on the time he spent at the college, remembering past incidents in a generalised way, and eventually catches a train and leaves. On the train he tries to remember Dockery and fails. But what catches his imagination is the thought that, for the dates to be right, Dockery, whoever he was, must have had a son when only nineteen or twenty.

The protagonist does not get much further in his reverie for the moment, for he falls asleep, waking up when he has to change trains at Sheffield. At the station there he walks to the end of the platform and looks out over the railway lines, seeing them as an image of how lives come together and diverge again. He is thinking partly of the mysterious Dockery and himself, but also, as Larkin then tells us, of his own aloneness. He had thought himself reconciled to his aloneness but suddenly it appears in a different light when he contrasts himself with his fantasy of Dockery and what he must have been like.

Yet the fourth and fifth stanzas, although they show us the protagonist wrestling with these problems, come to no direct conclusion. Instead he is sidetracked into wondering about habit in general, how it is that he is in his position – 'no son, no wife, / No house or land' – while other people are in quite different positions. It has, he thinks, very little to do with our conscious ambitions and desires; rather, habit is something which happens to you, inexorably, throughout life, and it is only when it is too late that you realise how closely it has bound you into its web.

This sense of a weight – the 'sand-clouds' which bear us towards death – and the protagonist's reawakened sense of being alone combine in a powerful final **quatrain** which tells us that nothing can really reconcile us to the passing of time and the loss of hope. No matter, therefore, how we live our lives, all difference is reduced to sameness by the imminence of death, 'the only end of age'.

> This poem is a particularly fine example of the way in which Larkin manages to work ordinary rhythms of speech and thought into a subtle poetic structure. Consider, for example, the direct speech of the first stanza, or the sleepy reverie of the third.
>
> The heart of the poem is, appropriately, to be found in the image at its centre, that of the joining and parting lines. The 'strong / Unhindered moon' relates oddly to this **image**; after all, the way in which the moon is actually reflected in railway lines is in fragments,

and perhaps this **irony** is intended. At any rate the moon here stands for a kind of isolation which, in a certain light, may look proud and strong but in another can come to seem merely defensive.

Certainly the central character is himself defensive: his attempts to explain Dockery seem simultaneously to suggest how inapplicable all this is to himself, as if indeed he is trying to protect himself with numbness from the 'shock' of this sudden realisation of a descent into lonely old age. But there is, of course, no possibility of going back; we know this from the beginning when the protagonist tries to return to his old college room. The fact that the door is 'Locked' is given heavy emphasis by the position of the word, and the image of the locked door into the past recurs in the fifth stanza.

The structure towards the end becomes complicated as the protagonist's own thoughts, which have been wandering, become inexorably focused on the issues raised by Dockery – or rather, by his associations with Dockery, since it is one of the points of the poem that the identity of Dockery remains in doubt throughout. 'Not from what / We think truest, or most want to do' refers to the failure of our beliefs and desires; we may think we want certain things, but we are overtaken by 'habit', by a fixed style, although we can never see how this carapace was first formed.

The 'sand-clouds' are thick, choking, deathly, but they are each formed in our own image, our doom is in each case appropriate to something we cannot perceive in ourselves. The couplet 'Life is first boredom, then fear. / Whether or not we use it, it goes' has a curiously jaunty rhythm, as though the protagonist is trying to revert to the carelessness he has known earlier; but this last attempt at a defence against death fails at the end, as we are made to realise the fallibility and impotence of our reason and our will.

Dean college official
death-suited 1) black-suited, formally dressed; 2) dressed as for a funeral – Dockery's?; 3) apt for death
half-tight half-drunk
who was killed in the Second World War, we may presume

COMMENTARIES HIGH WINDOWS

> **Sheffield** a Northern town here being used as an image of industry as opposed to the peacefulness of the college
>
> **warp** become stuck, usually through damp
>
> **patronage** Larkin is here suggesting that, just as for some people a growing son reminds them of their own age, so for him this growing sense of 'nothing' occupies a parallel role – or a worse one?

HIGH WINDOWS   (FROM HIGH WINDOWS)

Appears to be about freedom – about the possibility of emerging from a stifling late-Victorian world of conventions and rules into the sunlight of sexual and moral liberation. In fact the argument in it is far more complex than that, culminating in one of Larkin's most memorable images

At first reading this is one of the most baffling of Larkin's poems, because it concludes with an **image** – the image, furthermore, which he uses again as the title of a collected volume – which, although beautiful and resonant in itself, appears to have very little connection with the main body of the poem.

The **protagonist** is an ageing man reflecting on the generation gap. He sees two young people and guesses that they have sexual relations, something which would have been unthinkable when he was their age. He says he knows this freedom is desirable ('paradise'); but when he talks about the 'happiness' of 'everyone young', one wonders whether he is not projecting some of his own feelings into the youngsters.

He seems to take a rueful pleasure in being part of a generation which is being 'pushed to one side', and then thinks back to his own youth and wonders whether the older generation then looked upon his generation with this half-**ironic** envy. And it is this thought which seems to lead him into the final image, the image of 'high windows'.

> We immediately notice the contrast in the poem between at least two registers of language. The vocabulary of the first stanza and of parts of the fourth is crude, even violent: this in part reflects the protagonist's own feelings, although perhaps he is disguising this by pretending inside himself that this is the kind of language which the young themselves use.

The last stanza, however, seems entirely different, confronting us with the problem of what these 'high windows' are. They conjoin an image of freedom – the 'deep blue air' – with a sense of exclusion from it; the reader is reminded of a nineteenth-century schoolroom, where the windows would be placed high off the ground so that no distractions from the outside world were felt. There is also a subsidiary connotation of church windows, 'high' in the other sense.

What connects the poem together, then, is Larkin's sense that although he is in the presence of something called freedom, he is never able to share in it except vicariously; perhaps this is the plight of the poet.

Notice the image of the outdated combine harvester, the piece of farm machinery left to rust in the fields. The passage in italics, representing the voice of a past older generation, speaks of religious fears and conventions which have now been brushed aside, left to rot; although this appears to refer to a time 'forty years back', perhaps it also refers to a voice which is still present in Larkin's mind, the voice of a guilt which is the inverse side, as it were, of free love.

The 'long slide' suggests an absence of restraint; these young people have freed themselves of parental and religious constraints, and yet perhaps the idea that they have done so successfully is itself fantasy.

This brings us back to the last stanza, for although we may interpret this as an exclusion from freedom, the image itself remains one of astonishing beauty, and perhaps there is a hint of a different, further meaning which is that complete freedom is unreal. Perhaps it is better to experience freedom in this bounded way, through the 'high windows'; perhaps the 'framing' of freedom within conventions might in the end be more satisfying than a total freedom which may end up, as in the vocabulary of the first stanza, by valuing nothing and providing no shape to the 'long slide'.

pills contraceptive pills
diaphragm a female contraceptive device
sun-comprehending Larkin appears to mean that the glass 'comprehends' the sun in the sense of understanding it, but also includes or frames it

ANNUS MIRABILIS   (FROM HIGH WINDOWS)

Again Larkin reflects on the generation gap as it appears to him, and particularly on changes in social mores and what they might mean to an older man observing changes in habits and practices of which he does not feel a part

This poem, like 'High Windows', is a reflection on the generation gap and on the sudden changes in the behaviour of young people which occurred during the 1960s. At first sight it seems to take a jaunty, carefree approach to the subject, as evidenced in the **choric** repetitions of the first and last stanzas and in the rhythm structure throughout.

The **persona** flippantly points out in the first stanza that although life has changed for many people as a result of the breaking down of social mores, he is rather too old for these changes to affect him and is thus left out. In the second stanza he contrasts the contemporary notions of free love with the situation between the sexes in the past, in his own youth, where everything sexual was coloured by 'shame' and was thus reduced to 'A sort of bargaining' in which each potential partner tried to get what they wanted by underhand means.

On the face of it he is glad this time has passed and that the 'quarrel', the difference between the wishes of boys and girls, men and women, has been resolved; but in the third stanza his **images** become so strong – 'A quite unlosable game' – that one cannot avoid feeling that there is **irony** here and that therefore the tone of 'life was never better' (itself a version of the famous slogan 'You never had it so good', coined in the 1960s by Prime Minister Harold Macmillan) is not merely celebratory but also a kind of warning to the young, and to society at large, that this kind of self-satisfied pleasure might well be only a prelude to something much worse.

To say that 'Sexual intercourse began / In nineteen sixty-three' is obviously ironic; what Larkin means is, first, that it again became possible to speak publicly about sex at that time, and second, that young people of the time have the illusion that, because of this, they are the inventors of sexual pleasure. The lifting of the ban on D. H. Lawrence's novel, *Lady Chatterley's Lover*, was a milestone in the relaxation of censorship. The pop group The Beatles were widely regarded as the first incarnation of this new, freer spirit of the 1960s.

The second stanza gives a sour picture of the past, looking back to the post-war years of austerity in economic and moral terms. The contrast between this and the succeeding stanza is crucial. The past is made to represent a 'wrangle', a struggle for scarce economic and emotional resources within the constraints of a non-expanding world, whereas the present is seen as a time when restraints have been lifted, when everybody can be a winner. Obviously, although perhaps it took a poet to realise what economists and politicians of the time refused to realise, a condition in which everybody wins is an illusion, and Larkin means us to notice this. So we recognise in the imagery of 'A brilliant breaking of the bank, / A quite unlosable game' the self-delusion of the gambler, an inability to realise that such a condition is bound to be a purely temporary one.

Therefore the final stanza is open to two different interpretations. On one level the protagonist seems quite content to rest within this illusion, rueful though his sense of his own age may be; on a deeper level, he is calling the reader's attention to the short-sightedness of this view and inviting us to criticise it.

The rhythms of the poem are intended to suggest the lyrics of a pop song, with its emphasis on instant pleasure; thus the popular tone of the poem is in ironic contrast to its Latin title, meaning 'Year of Wonders'.

LP long-playing record (itself a new medium in the 1960s)

SAD STEPS   (FROM HIGH WINDOWS)

In part, a parody of 'romantic' meditation on the moon; instead of being a stimulus to wide-ranging thought and emotion, the moon for the protagonist ends up as a sad reminder of the ageing process

The poem begins in typically Larkin fashion, with a slang phrase which is immediately contrasted with a different world represented by the 'moon's cleanliness'. This unexpected second world seems initially to provoke some genuine feeling in the poet as he describes a transformed nightworld of 'wedge-shadowed gardens' under a 'cavernous, a wind-picked sky'. But we as readers are not allowed to reside in this transformed realm, or, therefore, in the possibility of poetic or visionary transformation at all. Instead, the powerful images are deflated as the poet asserts that there is 'something laughable about this', although precisely what is laughable is not easy to discern.

At all events, as the third and fourth stanzas develop the **symbolic** qualities of the moon – particularly its 'separateness', its removal from the realm of humanity – come to be seen as in some sense 'preposterous', and this becomes a self-fulfilling prophecy as the poet makes his series of **ironic** exclamations. These pronouncements – 'Lozenge of love!' and so on – he concludes to be ridiculous, beside the point, the products of an overheated imagination; instead, he asserts, the sight of the moon, its 'hardness' and 'brightness', only really serves to point up the contrast with the processes of gradual attrition that represent life here below.

> Like many of Larkin's poems, 'Sad Steps' begins by setting itself in a profoundly recognisable, everyday scene, and one which already at the beginning of the poem undercuts or downplays the status and viewpoint of the protagonist. Yet there is a continual oscillation in the poem between the ridiculousness he appears to represent and the much deeper qualities that he evidences – in, for example, the beautifully formed **imagery** of the fourth and fifth lines – and it is this oscillation that can be taken as the heart of the poem.

> We might feel as readers that we are challenged, at least at the beginning, to take sides. Do we share the proffered feeling that there is 'something laughable' about this – about the moon, or perhaps more accurately about any inflated, symbolic relation or response to the moon? Or are we more impressed with the poetic accuracy of the 'wind-picked sky', and thus perhaps rather impatient with the constantly deflationary, mocking tone that pervades parts of the poem? More, perhaps, to the point: do we actually *believe* this second voice, or do we find that it is a voice of self-delusion, the voice of one who does not *want* to believe, or to be seen to believe, in the possibilities of transcendence – because, perhaps, he finds the implications too frightening?

> There is, after all, a great deal in the poem that suggests that there is something here that is really not laughable at all but, on the contrary,

too big to deal with. 'Cavernous'; 'Immensements'; the 'wide stare': whatever tone these words might variously reflect, the fact remains that the poem does indeed convey with remarkable skill the sense of distant deeps and skies, even while it professes to dismiss any such possibility.

There are, of course, the slight 'shivers' of the fifth stanza, but this is a typically guarded phrase. It may mean that, even for the well-defended personality, there may be moments of illumination that force one to shiver in fear or awe despite oneself; but it could equally be that the protagonist is simply growing cold; or, thirdly, that he would, if asked, explain his shiver as due to the chill even while knowing, in some part of himself, this to be untrue.

The ending of the poem seems not so much to resolve the principal dilemma – the question of whether a romantic view of the world is sustainable or is merely a deflection from the ever-presence of the commonplace – but rather to move it in a slightly different direction, back inside the **protagonist**. It is now a meditation not on the lostness of the human species in the depths of space, the grandeur of the universe, and the possibility of an adequate emotional and verbal response to such grandeur, but rather on mortality and ageing.

There is something even more curious about the ending. The whole poem is constructed of **pentameters**, although some of the lines (such as lines six, eleven and thirteen) only just stretch themselves to five stresses and could, in a different context, be read as **tetrameters**. It is also the case that all the lines end on a stress – but not the final one which, although a pentameter, ends on a weak syllable. This makes the closing of the poem oddly difficult to read; but it also seems to suggest that perhaps this apparent ending is not quite an ending at all. The poem tails off rather than coming to any resolution. This, one might say, intensifies the tone of regret that runs throughout – intensifies it **paradoxically** through 'weakness', through resistance to a simple summary that might resolve the conflicts and antagonisms of the poem.

Immensements Larkin's own word, coined to demonstrate an artificially inflated poetic perception

COMMENTARIES — THE EXPLOSION

THE EXPLOSION (FROM HIGH WINDOWS)

Recounts the legend that, at the very moment of a mine explosion, the wives of the miners had a vision of their dying husbands

This is an extraordinarily moving poem about an explosion in a coalmine, and more specifically about a rumour that at the moment of the explosion, in which many miners died, their wives at home knew it was happening and saw visions of their husbands. The rhythms are unusual for Larkin, conjuring up a kind of solemn processional, emphasised in particular by the Church text which constitutes the sixth stanza.

Larkin begins by imagining an ominous state of quiet. He presents to us the miners: they are rough, loud, but vital; although they work underground, they still have some contact with the world of nature, shown by the reference to rabbits and larks' eggs, and they retain a gentleness, evidenced in the lodging of the eggs in the grasses.

Their passing through the gates is literally their entry into the works of the mine, but **symbolically** we are also reminded of an entry into death's kingdom. The only outward sign of the explosion deep underground is a 'tremor', and the deaths are only registered by the cows who stop chewing 'for a second'. But this movement is reflected at a different level by the entry into the poem of a solemn moment from a funeral service.

This text, however, is not merely inserted by the poet; it is also said to have been part of the set of visions seen by the womenfolk. They saw the text, and they saw their husbands, already dead, walking towards them, larger than life. Larkin makes no attempt to explain this extraordinary phenomenon.

> This poem is very rare among Larkin's works in being entirely free from irony. It is a solemn, sad poem which recounts to us a mystery and is content to leave any explanation of that mystery to us.
>
> The **imagery** is closely worked: notice, for example, how the closeness of an entire community, soon to be shattered by death, is indicated in a single line, 'Fathers, brothers, nicknames, laughter', which shades from the factual into a lightly-sketched account of how the men relate to each other, suggesting that they have all been related since birth, that they know each other beyond words.

THE EXPLOSION   COMMENTARIES

The 'Shadows' and the sleeping 'slagheap' of the first stanza are tied by alliteration to the 'sun' of stanza five, and 'Scarfed as in a heat-haze'. What is conjured up here is a sense of sleeping which is disturbed only lightly by the tremendous and violent events below the ground, which in turn emphasises the strangeness and inexplicability of the women's visions.

We see much of the imagery drawn together in the last full stanza and the floating last line. In death these men are 'Larger than in life', creating a contrast with the belittling effect of life as a miner, and this sense is further emphasised by the phrase 'they managed', as though even when alive these men only just managed to live, financially as well as in terms of the everyday risks which miners run. 'Gold as on a coin' indicates the way in which these men – during life blackened and debased as in the second stanza – can only be transformed by death into something of value; perhaps it is only through the shock of something like this explosion that mine-owners can be brought to realise the human value of their workers. The word 'Somehow' emphasises the way in which the women themselves were not concerned, or able, to make sense of their visions, thus contributing to a suggestion that they were real and not, for example, imagined for the sake of gain. The unbroken eggs are a powerful image of gentleness, care, a summary of all the virtues of community, marriage, life together which have been shattered by this explosion and by those responsible for it.

moleskins thick trousers worn in the countryside
scarfed wrapped; here also, perhaps, protected from the violence below

THE CARD-PLAYERS   (FROM HIGH WINDOWS)

Seems to attempt to reconjure the curious mixture of solemnity and profanity which is typical of seventeenth-century Dutch painting

Like 'The Explosion' this is an unusual poem for Larkin, although for quite different reasons. It is an attempt to call to mind, or reconstruct, a painting

COMMENTARIES THE CARD-PLAYERS

from a very particular period, a seventeenth-century Dutch painting, and the way in which Larkin portrays his characters is designed to correspond very closely to the heavy, clumping, rural tones of this kind of art.

The names of the characters are invented so as to combine **stereotypical** Dutch spelling with meanings which are obscene in English. The observer of the poem sees this scene of drunkenness, gambling and swearing, but he has a double reaction. Perhaps this is well summarised in the image of Old Prijck's 'skull face' being 'firelit': the face like a skull belongs to the world of death, cold, the dark, whereas the firelight which illuminates this imagined interior belongs to the world of life, warmth, colour. The protagonist seems to see the scene as loathsome in its animality, yet to be envied for the unquestioning communal warmth which it possesses.

This doubleness of mind is well conjured in the final, 'The secret, bestial peace!', where the protagonist seems to be admiring, envying and despising all at the same time. All of these emotions are, obviously, directed at the kind of bucolic scene he is depicting and which can be found in Dutch painting, but they are also, perhaps, directed at painting and thus art itself in a general way, which is 'secret' and 'bestial' in the ways in which it moves people without their knowledge or acquiescence.

> The principal conflict in this poem is between opposing attitudes on the part of the **persona** himself. His contempt is clearly shown in the opening two lines. This is a world of animal impulse, bestial drunkenness, mindless sinking into degraded behaviour. Even the identities of the people are not secure: 'someone behind drinks ale', as though there are many other Jans and Dirks, all undifferentiated.
>
> But there is more here than contempt, and this hinges particularly on the **symbol** of the cards. At the surface level these are simply playing-cards on which to gamble, but we sense below this a relationship between the cards and the stereotyped characters in the painting, so that we are reminded of the tarot pack.
>
> Notice that as soon as 'Dirk deals the cards' we are moved, as if by magic, out from the hot interior to the 'surrounding starlessness', as though there is something in the cards which reminds us of a greater and more frightening world far away from the comforts of home.

THE CARD-PLAYERS   COMMENTARIES

The word 'starlessness' perhaps also serves to remind us of the directionlessness of man: how he would 'follow the star' if he could, even by practising astrology, but in this condition of 'starlessness' there are only the cards to turn to.

But perhaps we do not want to wander out into this dubious, dark world; perhaps we would sooner stay in our cave, which represents home, in which we can be shielded, if only for a time, from the terrifying knowledge of the outside. And perhaps, therefore, this is what painting is for, to shield us from a journey outside.

That outside may be populated by the eternal forms represented by 'Rain, wind and fire'; but in here, in the world of home and maybe also in the world of vicarious, aesthetic pleasure, there is instead 'The secret, bestial peace' which proffers its own values and suffers us its own enjoyments.

Hogspeuw pun on 'hog', a male pig, and 'spew' meaning 'to vomit'
Dogstoerd pun on 'dog' and 'turd', meaning 'excrement'
clay meaning 'clay pipe'
Prijck pun on 'prick', slang word for 'penis'
ham-hung with hams hanging from them
gobs slang for 'spits'

THIS BE THE VERSE   (FROM HIGH WINDOWS)

> Appears to suggest that the generations pass down all the wrong things to each other, and that therefore it would be better not to have children at all than to risk doing to them what has been done to oneself

This strange poem has become one of Larkin's most famous; perhaps its brevity and simplicity make it peculiarly memorable.

Bringing together themes from, for example, 'Dockery and Son' and 'High Windows', Larkin here explores the question of what the generations pass on to one another yet again, but there is an unrelieved bleakness to this poem which sets it apart from many earlier ones. The tone is set in the first line, and intensifies in the second stanza where, first, we are told that this pain in the transition between the generations is nothing new but the inescapable stuff of history, and second, we are treated to the voice of casualness, the tones of a poetic **persona** for whom the past holds nothing but a prefiguration of the awfulness of the present.

The third stanza seems to start with a grand generalisation, 'Man hands on misery to man', and the solemnity of this is increased by the smoothly beautiful rhythms of the second line; but this poeticising is deliberately wrecked by the crudity and violence of the last two lines.

> What are we really to make of poems like this, which sound unrelievedly pessimistic? Certainly they cannot be saved from this pessimism, but we can look more closely at Larkin's stance here by noting the relation between the poem and its title.
>
> The title suggests religion, a lesson read out at Sunday-morning service, whereas the poem itself exists in an inexorably secular world. This tension is part of the point: just as the world of religion constitutes a critique of everyday reality, so the ordinary world mocks religious pretensions. What is important is the misfit between religion, ideals, codes of moral behaviour, value systems, on the one hand, and on the other, the casual valuelessness implicit in this poem and also, as Larkin sees it, in most of the secularised world around him.
>
> What this moves towards is a real nihilism whereby the only answer to the great questions of life comes in the form of the petty, crude **aphorism**, 'Get out as early as you can, / And don't have any kids yourself'. It is not so much the advice which is shocking but the *tone* of the advice, which makes it sound as though life is not only not worth living, it is not even worthy of serious, thoughtful comment.

soppy-stern Larkin's own compound, including strictness and sentimentality
coastal shelf the shallow waters around a coastline, which suddenly give way to the ocean depths a certain distance out

GOING, GOING (FROM HIGH WINDOWS)

The poet regrets the passing of aspects of a traditional England: the disappearance of the countryside, the encroachments of industry and suburbia, the replacement of accepted values by a kind of rootlessness which tends inevitably towards the destructive

This is a meditative poem, although with Larkin the term 'meditative' often seems too strong for what *looks* like a stream of random reflections.

The main subject is the disappearance of England's countryside. The poet begins by saying that, on the whole, he has always thought that the countryside, and some kind of balance between the rural and the urban, would survive for his lifetime. He has known that traditional ways of life are under threat, but he has assumed that these threats were for the most part 'false alarms'; and even if the sprawl of the suburbs does increase, he has assumed – selfishly – that he and people like him would still be able to find the countryside by driving out to it.

In the third stanza he moves to a generalisation, that 'nature' is stronger, more resilient than man; that however we may damage it with pollution and other forms of carelessness, it will always somehow be able to clear itself and recover.

At the end of this stanza, however, he registers a change of feeling, although he is unable to say clearly why that change has occurred. Does he increasingly doubt the ability of nature to survive the onslaughts on it, or is it simply that he is growing older? At any event he sees the rising generation as marked by an increasing greed and by an increasing emphasis on profit at the expense of care for the environment – the 'ten / Per cent more in the estuaries' is more pollution, more refuse, more sludge. To the poet this appears as a speeding up of the process whereby everything will end up 'bricked in', except for parts of the country preserved for the sake of tourism. All that will remain of England will be memories and those bits and pieces which will survive in museums; for the people, there will be a world composed of 'concrete and tyres'.

In the last stanza he gloomily points out that probably nobody really intends this to happen, but then, intention is not necessary; already things have drifted a very long way, and he thinks that there is nothing to prevent them from drifting further still.

GOING, GOING

The title refers to the language of the auctioneer who, when selling something to the highest bidder, will say 'Going … going … gone' before the hammer comes down. This suggests the image of parts of the country being sold off to those who can pay most, with no regard for the social cost.

The rhythm is fast, apparently casual, reflecting the carelessness which the poet sees all around him. Some of the stanzas flow into each other without due regard for the endings of lines and this is deliberate. We see reflected the sense of an unstoppable drift or flow away from a more orderly, responsible society towards one where nothing is planned and no account is taken of people's real needs.

He feels rueful about the passing away of an older order: in the first stanza he clearly does not admire the 'louts', yet they represent a more communal world where everybody had their place, and are thus perhaps preferable to the screaming children of the fourth stanza. The 'bleak high-risers' of the second stanza are blocks of flats, but also the people who live in them, whose outlook is bleak.

At the beginning of the third stanza he uses the word 'just' in two ways: in terms of obvious clause structure it connects with the second line, but the first line including 'just' is also an entity in its own right, suggesting the precarious balance between nature and man and how easily that balance may be overturned.

Throughout the poem Larkin refuses to attribute simple blame for this condition. 'The crowd … in the M1 café' may offend him in many ways, but their taste, or lack of it, is not their own fault. We get nearer to the heart of the cause of the imminent catastrophe in the fifth stanza, where the 'spectacled grins' represent the blandness of businessmen as they contemplate a commercial manoeuvre without taking account of the possible human consequences. What is important here is the fact that these are indeed mere 'grins', not whole people.

The phrase 'Grey area grants' is bitter with **irony**. What Larkin is saying is that successive governments have failed to maintain 'green areas', places where industry and commerce should not be allowed to interfere with the environment; all we can do now is to allow industry yet more expansion and thus convert the green into grey – and worse, help industry to move there because it will save them expense.

Larkin determinedly refuses to convert his observations into a political analysis. In the sixth stanza he takes up the position of the ordinary observer. He does not bother to complete the sentence about getting to the sea because he assumes everybody will know what he is referring to: the traffic jams, the pollution, the commercialisation. And he follows this up by insisting that this is just his personal impression: 'It seems, just now'.

The last line of the seventh stanza is hard to make out: does Larkin really mean that England is in the hands of 'crooks and tarts', or does he mean that this is the *impression* England now gives? Perhaps he means to leave the question open.

'The shadows, the meadows, the lanes' summarise the countryside but are perhaps also a reference to the great artist of rural England, John Constable.

In the last stanza he equates motivations – 'greeds' – and their effects – 'garbage' – to intensify his argument, but returns in the last line to insist that this is just his individual, amateurish perception. The strength of this formulation is that he means to remind us that, really, he is not alone in this feeling: that many of us, with similar unsystematic impotence, share it.

split-level shopping shopping malls
M1 the first motorway in Britain
Business Page in a newspaper
estuaries areas of water at the mouths of rivers
snuff it colloquial (and casual) for 'dying'
the whole / Boiling a slang expression for 'the whole thing'
crooks and tarts criminals and prostitutes; but the half-jocular terms suggest to us that their criminality is not to be taken too seriously
guildhalls here, medieval civic buildings
carved notice that, in accordance with the rhythm, this should be read here as a two-syllable word, itself a relevant archaism
choirs here, short for 'choir-stalls'

THE BUILDING (FROM HIGH WINDOWS)

About a hospital; also about our wish to resist death, the feebleness of that wish, and the way in which the separate world of the hospital prefigures the final separation

Like 'Essential Beauty', this poem depends initially on tension between the description and the location; we are in a hospital, but Larkin lets the fact dawn on us gradually.

Initially the building is presented as a thing of beauty, a 'lucent comb' which is (notice the **alliteration**) 'Higher than the handsomest hotel'. At the end we are offered another image, the 'clean-sliced cliff', which suggests the correlation between the building and the precipice of death; what, we are therefore asked, is all this building for when our own lives might collapse in a moment?

In the first stanza we are invited to contrast the apparent modernity of the hospital with the surrounding streets 'out of the last century', and throughout the poem we can reflect on a contrast between efficiency and scruffiness. The language used shows Larkin at his most brilliant, impersonating the everyday reader with **colloquial** and imprecise phrases like 'tea at so much a cup' and 'ripped mags'.

He also impersonates the person attending hospital who does not properly understand what is going on — which is, after all, our usual condition in a hospital, whether we are recognisably ill or not. Thus at the end of the second stanza 'a kind of nurse' arrives; she picks out somebody from the waiting room, apparently at random, just as death will take us at random and without explanation.

In the fourth stanza this innocence about the purposes of hospitals increases as we are invited to suppose that the grandeur of the hospital, its obvious costliness, reflects how seriously we may have 'gone wrong', as though we were machines which can only be understood or, we hope, repaired by a skilled mechanic.

Larkin picks out, as in the 'Toads' poems, the sense of how odd it is, on a working day, to be in an unusual place, and yet how suspiciously we view those similarly picked out: 'how their eyes / Go to each other, guessing'. He also emphasises throughout the peculiar solemnity of being in hospital — e.g. 'They're quiet' — partly out of individual fear, partly from a realisation that this condition of being sick is something which all of us will come to in the end.

The outside world seems approachable, yet in hospital we are held away from it. It is remarkable, Larkin says, how quickly the world of the ordinary, where 'girls with hair-dos fetch / Their separates from the cleaners', becomes a foreign place while we take up our place in the ranks of the sick, the malfunctioning.

Being in hospital obliterates all distinction of age, of gender: 'All know they are going to die'. It is not, of course, that everybody is going to die in this hospital, but that being in hospital reminds us, if only temporarily, of the inescapability of death. And yet, Larkin suggests at the end, the hospital also reminds us of all the effort put into the 'struggle to transcend', the effort to postpone at least – although nothing can possibly do this, least of all the act represented in the final, floating line, of visiting the sick with 'wasteful, weak, propitiatory flowers'.

> The flowers at the end are 'propitiatory' because they are intended, unconsciously, to stave off, to postpone the operations of physical sickness, to propitiate the gods. There is a sense throughout the poem that the modern concept of medicine is only a small part of the purpose of hospitals; that the deeper purpose is to erect some kind of building, some **symbol** of the solid and even the soaring in the face of the inevitability of physical decline. The hospital becomes almost a magical place, although it is doubtful whether this magic is effective.
>
> The first stanza portrays the faulty body as a breathing chest, sighing in its uncertainty. This superhuman image is immediately contrasted with the 'scruffy' porters and the ambulances, the frightening smell, all too physical reminders of the physical reality of the hospital. The key contrast throughout is between the everyday normality of 'paperbacks, and tea at so much a cup' and death; Larkin emphasises the state of terrified docility into which we are put by our encounters with sickness, our own or others': we are 'those who tamely sit'.
>
> The word 'Humans' erupts into the third stanza unexpectedly, reminding us of what we all have in common, even though we may not want to be reminded of it; for what we have in common is mortality, which constitutes a 'ground curiously neutral'. The phrase

'how tall / It's grown by now' has at least three meanings: it refers to the hospital, to our anxiety at being there, and to the disease which may be growing inside us.

The notion of confession in the fourth stanza is important, suggesting as it does that the hospital, even medicine as a whole practice, may now occupy a place in people's lives similar to the place occupied by the Church in past ages – a point emphasised and refined by the image of the 'cathedrals' towards the end. It is as though the hospital has become the best we can do in terms of offering something to the powers of life and death. The phrase 'as they climb / To their appointed levels' again invokes the **ironic** comparison between the hospital and religion: this is indeed a heaven or a hell in which we find ourselves, especially in the sense that there is nothing we can do as individuals to avoid our fate. The notion of 'rooms past those' and so on intensifies this image by reminding us of Dante's circles of hell, from which there is no escape.

A contrast, then, is being pointed here between the mundanity of illness and the sacred aura with which death might be surrounded, beneficially or otherwise, in other cultures: this is further emphasised by the **apostrophe** 'O world, / Your loves, your chances' which suggests how inappropriate any sort of romanticising might be to the facts of sickness, especially when considered on a mass scale.

The 'unseen congregations' return us to the problematic relation between the hospital and the Church: clearly in the hospital the coming of death is celebrated as a sort of ritual, but is it the right sort? Or are we reduced by modern mass medicine to a condition of passivity in which we cannot understand even our own passing?

lucent shining, bright
comb Larkin means to compare the many-windowed hospital to a honeycomb
lagged covered, probably rather shabbily, to prevent loss of heat
hair-dos the implication is of cheap, standardised ways of arranging the hair
separates Larkin is using the **jargon** of sellers and cleaners of clothes to refer to skirts, blouses, etc (note the term picked up in 'separately' five lines further on)

AUBADE   (IN THE *TIMES LITERARY SUPPLEMENT*, 1977)

This stately and impressive poem is one of Larkin's clearest and most sustained attempts to portray and come to grips with the fear of death

The first stanza of 'Aubade' asserts the difference between two 'visions': the vision of the day-time world on the one hand, and on the other that perception in which 'I see what's really always there', a perception particularly acute in the small hours of the morning. What this 'truer' perception sees is one thing and one thing only: 'Unresting death' – 'unresting' in the sense that, first, it is relentless in its dealings with man, and second, it prevents any possibility of real 'rest' for any of us. The fear of death fills the mind, driving all other thoughts away, and although it is a topic which endlessly recurs, it still possesses a vivid and ever-fresh power to 'hold and horrify'.

In the second stanza the poet begins a list of those aspects of death which are sometimes claimed to be determining factors in our anxiety about it but which, to the poet, are mere deflections from the full horror he is trying to express. He is not concerned with remorse; nor is he concerned with the shortness of time one may have; or with how things in one's past life have gone wrong or not given one sufficient chances of success or happiness: none of these are significant, he says. Rather what matters is the sheer 'extinction', the negation of being that death represents.

This, the poet says, is the source of our real fear, and it is precisely this fear that the whole ensemble of religion has been constructed to avoid. Theological promises of immortality are a mere charade; neither can we make ourselves feel any better by using the philosophical argument that we cannot be afraid of something we cannot imagine, and will not in any obvious sense experience even when it occurs. Instead, it is precisely this unknown quality, and the consequent abolition of all human coordinates, that form the very substance of our fear.

It is, the fourth stanza says, the ineluctability of death that terrifies us, the certainty of its advent, the impossibility of defeating or postponing it. In the face of these matters, it makes no difference whether we approach death with 'Courage' or cowardice; there is nothing noble or honourable, Larkin says, about confronting death, for it will have no effect at all.

COMMENTARIES   AUBADE

In the fifth stanza the day begins to break in upon these night-time meditations, but the knowledge of death does not disappear, it is not dissolved in the growing daylight, rather it 'stands plain as a wardrobe', even though such knowledge is itself a tissue of impossibilities. The daytime world returns; but it has to exist *alongside* this darker knowledge, so that even the comparative normality of the postmen doing their rounds is tainted by this other knowledge and they come to seem more 'like doctors', those other reminders of mortality and vulnerability.

An aubade is in classical tradition a song sung at – and normally in celebration of – dawn; the word, however, derives from the Latin word for 'white', and it is no accident that the day that finally breaks – ominously – at the end of the poem shows us a sky 'white as clay, with no sun', in a savage **parody** of the beauty of the dawn.

Structurally, this poem is one of Larkin's masterpieces. Each ten-line stanza is **end-stopped**, and consists of nine pentameters with a trimeter as the ninth line. These shorter lines serve the function – through their rhyme with the line before – of a kind of echo or repetition, which strengthens the poem's feeling of inevitability.

Many of the **pentameters** are **iambic**, but there are plenty of variations. The seventh line of the first stanza, for example – 'And where and when I shall myself die' – lacks a ninth syllable, which inserts a hiatus before the final word, thus strongly emphasising 'die' as the conclusion to the line and to the sentence. The final line of the second stanza, by contrast, is over-long, carrying a number of weak syllables. Perhaps the most startling effect comes in the final stanza, in the line about the sky which is quoted above: here again there is an omitted syllable towards the end, but the effect is different and is to suggest equal emphasis on all the last three syllables – 'with no sun' – bringing out the horror of the image with tremendous force.

blanks goes blank
brocade a particularly ornate kind of cloth associated with tapestries
come round regain consciousness

71

Part three

Extended commentaries

Poem 1   Ambulances

Closed like confessionals, they thread
Loud noons of cities, giving back
None of the glances they absorb.
Light glossy grey, arms on a plaque,
They come to rest at any kerb:
All streets in time are visited.

Then children strewn on steps or road,
Or women coming from the shops
Past smells of different dinners, see
A wild white face that overtops
Red stretcher-blankets momently
As it is carried in and stowed,

And sense the solving emptiness
That lies just under all we do,
And for a second get it whole,
So permanent and blank and true.
The fastened doors recede. *Poor soul*,
They whisper at their own distress;

For borne away in deadened air
May go the sudden shut of loss
Round something nearly at an end,
And what cohered in it across
The years, the unique random blend
Of families and fashions, there

At last begin to loosen. Far
From the exchange of love to lie
Unreachable inside a room
The traffic parts to let go by
Brings closer what is left to come,
And dulls to distance all we are.

This is a poem that 'threads' its way between the particular and the general. Although it purports to be representing a repeating event – the passage of the ambulance through traffic, its arrival at 'any kerb' – and thus deals largely, at least to begin with, in plurals, we also get a vivid sense of a specific scene which is being depicted.

The first stanza describes the ambulance itself. The essential point about it, as the poet sees it, is that it is 'Closed', it repels enquiry or investigation. Inside it, something entirely private is occurring: this privacy is likened to the privacy of the confessional in order to show the ambulance as a sequestered space. Perhaps the ambulance, like the confessional, also represents something sacred, some mystery which is inexplicable to the outer world.

The second stanza concentrates on the people who see the ambulance's arrival. What is crucial to this portrayal is the emphasis on how *random* their presence is; they have not gathered or congregated to look at the ambulance, they have indeed had no foreknowledge of its arrival, the children are 'strewn' haphazardly, the women are merely 'coming from the shops'. Into this world, however, something totally different is inserted, the 'wild white face', white with sickness, or loss of blood, or surprise, or shock – we as readers know no more than the watchers on the street.

But in the third stanza Larkin suggests that, despite the apparent randomness of the event, something significant is conveyed or achieved by the arrival of the ambulance, some realisation of what he refers to as the 'solving emptiness'. As in 'Days', the word 'solving' carries connotations both of solution and dissolution, as though this 'emptiness' is both the answer to all our questions and simultaneously the end to questioning itself.

The fourth stanza, which is quite complexly structured, is mainly about the person who is being 'borne away', about how that person – like any other individual – was a 'unique random blend', had been composed of his or her own family history, experiences, hopes and fears. The stress is on the fact that it is this particular person who is being taken away, and any individual is simultaneously irreplaceable – to loved ones, friends, relations – and inconsequential, in terms of the greater order of things.

The fifth stanza, which is mostly a single long sentence, summarises what has been said so far by comparing the image of the ambulance itself and its journey to the wider journey through life towards its inevitable end.

One of Larkin's gifts, which this poem demonstrates with particular force, is his skill in the placement of tiny, everyday words. In the first stanza, for example, 'any kerb' immediately broadens out the reference of the poem to include the reader while at the same time underlining the way in which nobody is exempt from the potential visit of the ambulance.

Perhaps a more puzzling usage is the word 'different' in the second stanza. Why should it matter that these are 'different dinners' (aside from the **alliteration** of the two words)? Perhaps the main force of the word here includes an emphasis on the 'journey' which these women are making, which might prefigure the emphasis on journeys that comes to dominate the latter part of the poem; and also the randomness of their journey, which strengthens the point about the randomness of the ambulance's visit.

Notice also in the last line of this stanza that 'it', not 'he' or 'she', is 'carried in and stowed'; the immediate reference, of course, is to the 'wild white face', and it is quite proper to use the 'it', but nevertheless the word serves – as does the other word 'stowed', with its connotations of luggage or cargo – to emphasise the dehumanisation that has occurred, the way in which the human individual has, in this extremity, been reduced to a thing, an object of observation with no power or agency of its own.

What *is* the vision that seems to be granted in the third stanza? We might say that it is a vision of death, but perhaps it is something more than that: perhaps an even more unified and final sense of how, as it were, life 'fits into' death, an awareness of how small and trivial our concerns look when put up against the bleak, inescapable facts of physical change and decay. Under these circumstances, Larkin characteristically and depressingly – or, some would say, realistically – insists, it is not that we feel real sympathy with the other; it is more that we retreat into our own selfish fears and 'whisper' at our own 'distress'.

The poem begins with the word 'Closed'; here as we go through the poem we have the 'fastened doors' (not unlike the 'tight-shut' doors in 'Dockery and Son'); and in the fourth stanza we have the 'sudden shut of loss', even further emphasising the way in which the ambulance represents a separate world of its own and in doing so prefigures that other closed box, the coffin. The air through which the ambulance now moves, we notice, is 'deadened'. In one literal sense this may refer to the quiet or hush that might descend on people under these circumstances, but it seems also

EXTENDED COMMENTARIES · HERE

to signify a way in which the very air has been imbued with the deathly, with a reminding whiff of mortality.

The sentence that comprises almost the whole of the last stanza is so contorted that it may be helpful to lay it out in the form it would have in prose: 'to lie, unreachable [and] far from the exchange of love, inside a room [the ambulance] [which] the traffic parts [in order to] let [it] go by – [to lie thus] brings closer what is left to come [death] and dulls to distance all [that] we are [while still alive]'.

POEM 2 HERE

Swerving east, from rich industrial shadows
And traffic all night north; swerving through fields
Too thin and thistled to be called meadows,
And now and then a harsh-named halt, that shields
Workmen at dawn; swerving to solitude
Of skies and scarecrows, haystacks, hares and pheasants,
And the widening river's slow presence,
The piled gold clouds, the shining gull-marked mud,

Gathers to the surprise of a large town:
Here domes and statues, spires and cranes cluster
Beside grain-scattered streets, barge-crowded water,
And residents from raw estates, brought down
The dead straight miles by stealing flat-faced trolleys,
Push through plate-glass swing doors to their desires –
Cheap suits, red kitchen-ware, sharp shoes, iced lollies,
Electric mixers, toasters, washers, driers –

A cut-price crowd, urban yet simple, dwelling
Where only salesmen and relations come
Within a terminate and fishy-smelling
Pastoral of ships up streets, the slave museum,
Tattoo-shops, consulates, grim head-scarfed wives;
And out beyond its mortgaged half-built edges
Fast-shadowed wheat-fields, running high as hedges,
Isolate villages, where removed lives

> Loneliness clarifies. Here silence stands
> Like heat. Here leaves unnoticed thicken,
> Hidden weeds flower, neglected waters quicken,
> Luminously-peopled air ascends;
> And past the poppies bluish neutral distance
> Ends the land suddenly beyond a beach
> Of shapes and shingle. Here is unfenced existence:
> Facing the sun, untalkative, out of reach.

The first stanza sees the poet, as so frequently in Larkin, on a train journey. The train is going through fairly ragged country, 'through fields / Too thin and thistled to be called meadows': we are reminded of the physically degraded land that often surrounds railways, although here that degradation seems to spread farther in all directions. There is, however, a moment of hope and pleasure towards the end of the stanza, represented in the river, in the 'piled gold clouds', even the 'shining gull-marked mud'.

What this sense of growing anticipation leads up to in the second stanza is the appearance of a town, although Larkin's depiction, initially quite conventional and generalised – 'domes and statues, spires and cranes' – comes to focus more solidly on his view of the kind of life people are likely to live there. This is a town which is initially represented essentially as a shopping centre, and one where the goods are cheap.

We might then suspect that Larkin is seeing this vision of the urban as exploitative and crass, as he sometimes does elsewhere, but in fact we see in the third stanza that his perspective is more poised than that. This may be a 'cut-price crowd', but it is 'urban yet simple'. He is not representing the town here as some sophisticated alternative to the countryside, but he does go on to contrast the shopping centre to the other places in the town, presumably not in the centre, where these shoppers actually live. The town (as we should already have deduced from the 'widening river' and from other features of the description in the second stanza) is, or has been, a port; hence the nicely poised phrase about the 'fishy-smelling / Pastoral of ships up streets' and the other, port-related phrases that follow it.

However, the train and the poet move on from the town, returning to the countryside, but now to a countryside that seems almost mystically transfigured. Here there is thickening, flowering, quickening (in the sense of 'bringing to life'); the air is 'Luminously-peopled'. Yet beyond this there is something else again: the land 'ends', and beyond is 'unfenced existence', which might represent the sea, although this is left inexplicit. But whether the poet has arrived there – or even what it would mean to arrive there – is left hovering; this final vision is, after all, 'out of reach'.

The first stanza remarkably replicates the process of a train journey: the repetition of 'swerving' is particularly graphic, as we are brought to imagine the train moving round long wide bends. We see ourselves only partly observing the unremarkable country through which we are passing until our attention is arrested by a gathering of features which indicate that something new and different is about to come into view.

We are in the early morning, when things are coming into view anyway; but there is a double process here, as the dawn awakening of the scene is replicated by the poet's own awakening – to what he sees, certainly, but also increasingly to what he imagines about the people he observes. One might indeed fairly ask whether he actually sees the people of the town at all, or whether it is more that the sight of the town propels him into populating it in his imagination, fantasising about the lives lived within its confines.

We then come to see that there are, in a sense, two towns here. There is the 'new town', represented by the shopping centre and also by the 'raw estates'; and there is the older port, represented in, for example, the 'grain-scattered streets, barge-crowded water', which perhaps moves us decisively beyond current perception, seeming in the elegance of its phrasing to link us, however fragilely, with an older perception of ancient ports and harbours. It is as though one of these towns is superimposed on the other, although it cannot entirely obliterate its presence. It is interesting that Larkin uses the word 'pastoral' in the third stanza. Historically, 'pastoral' has referred to a certain vision of the countryside as a happy place of laughing shepherds and gambolling lambs; this, however, does not seem to be quite Larkin's meaning here, any more than either of the visions of the countryside he offers can be conveniently bounded by 'pastoral' notions.

A crucial – and difficult – passage occurs at the break between the third and fourth stanzas. 'Isolate' here should be read as an (unusual) adjective; the next five words would be rearranged in prose as 'where loneliness clarifies removed lives', with 'clarifies' as the verb and 'removed' as an adjective. After the bustle of the town, then, there is loneliness and silence; but as one looks more closely one sees that this apparent isolation is

HERE

EXTENDED COMMENTARIES

in fact thickly populated – not just with people, perhaps, but with all the panoply of nature.

But – and this is the essence of the complexity of the final stanza – there are limits to this clarification. The 'bluish neutral distance' which 'Ends the land' is, after all, not quite available to our perception; however much we may strain to make it clear, it remains vague and uncertain. And so we come to the final sentence. One way of reading it would be to say that, after all the complications of the relations between town centre, old town, suburb, countryside, there is something else; but what that something else might be remains tantalisingly inexplicit. Another way of reading this last sentence would place the emphasis where the title of the poem suggests we should, on 'Here'; the meaning would thus be that as we strive to be really 'here', wherever 'here' may be, as we strive to isolate and clarify what it is we are observing, or even where it is that we live, it continually slips away from us, refuses to describe itself ('untalkative') and remains in some sense ungraspable. The very notion 'Here', then, contains or enacts a **paradox**: even as we try to specify where 'Here' is, we are moved past it – on a train, indeed, but also on our metaphorical journey through life – and it remains intangible, always receding into a further distance.

POEM 3   TOADS REVISITED

Walking around in the park
Should feel better than work:
The lake, the sunshine,
The grass to lie on,

Blurred playground noises
Beyond black-stockinged nurses –
Not a bad place to be.
Yet it doesn't suit me,

Being one of the men
You meet of an afternoon:
Palsied old step-takers,
Hare-eyed clerks with the jitters,

Waxed-fleshed out-patients
Still vague from accidents,
And characters in long coats
Deep in the litter-baskets -

All dodging the toad work
By being stupid or weak.
Think of being them!
Hearing the hours chime,

Watching the bread delivered,
The sun by clouds covered,
The children going home;
Think of being them,

Turning over their failures
By some bed of lobelias,
Nowhere to go but indoors,
No friends but empty chairs -

No, give me my in-tray,
My loaf-haired secretary,
My shall-I-keep-the-call-in-Sir:
What else can I answer,

When the lights come on at four
At the end of another year?
Give me your arm, old toad;
Help me down Cemetery Road.

This poem, of course, develops from the poem called 'Toads', and in one sense is a reply to the argument raised there about why it is necessary to work.

Here the **persona** spends most of the poem toying with the idea of not working, and how it would feel. But the images he comes up with are curiously, and deliberately, empty. 'Walking around in the park' may sound pleasant in a way, but it is also purposeless, repetitive, without shape or design; and this is the main problem that the persona encounters, how to give shape to a life which is without work. 'Not a bad place to be' is rather weak advocacy; and indeed the people he encounters in the park are all weak, all people who obviously have proved unable to take the strain of life – very different, we notice, from the more envied outcasts of 'Toads'.

What all of these 'characters' have in common, says Larkin, is that they are 'All dodging the toad work', they are all 'stupid or weak'. But here again we encounter the problem we came across with 'Toads', which is about the level of **irony** in the poem. Are we meant to agree with the persona in his rather cursory assessment of the people in the park? Or are we meant to think that he is rationalising, preparing for himself suspect arguments about why it is better to go on working by claiming to despise those who do not? These people, he claims, are all passive: they watch the bread being delivered, they hear the clocks, they see those, like the children, who have places to be at fixed times. But they themselves can do nothing but reflect aimlessly on their 'failures'; they have no community to which to belong.

Faced with these **images**, the persona not surprisingly opts to return to the world of work (maybe simply to return to the office after a meditative lunch hour) and to settle back into a routine which, at least, gives one a sense of purpose in life. The force of the last image is to suggest that, when all comes down to dust, we all need some kind of comfort, a prop with which to get through the days. Work is just such a prop, and therefore, although we know that in one sense it will prove to be deadly, nevertheless it can help us on the unavoidable journey.

There is something determinedly casual about much of this poem, especially near the beginning where even the rhymes seem throwaway and lines like 'The grass to lie on' barely seem to say anything at all. Part of the point of this is to suggest that the persona's vision is itself 'blurred', like the background noises: he is not yet really focusing on the world of the park, and perhaps this is because he does not want to; he has no wish to face what the reality of not working would be like.

But during the third stanza the scene comes starkly to life with the 'Palsied old step-takers' and 'Hare-eyed clerks', as though the persona can no longer avoid the terror of these shapeless lives as they intrude upon him. The sense he is trying to conjure up here is like that which many of us have felt when excused from school through illness, yet able to move about. There is a pleasure at being released from everyday life but also a doubt, amounting in the case of the 'hare-eyed' clerks to an image of panic, about what to do with the time. And beyond this lies an image of sickness, the 'Waxed-fleshed out-patients'. The proximity of this image to that of the 'characters in long coats', the tramps looking for what they can find in rubbish bins, may also remind us of the people 'in their long coats' who come running across the fields in 'Days', and thus remind of the inevitability of sickness and death.

'The sun by clouds covered' is a curious line; it appears too 'poetic', too deliberately artificial to belong in such a colloquial discourse. Perhaps Larkin inserts it here to suggest reverie and meditation: to say that, yes, given this freedom it would be possible to drift away (like the clouds), but would we be able to stand that drifting away, the lack of conventional comforts and supports?

His irony returns in the rhyming of 'failures' and 'lobelias', which has the effect of reducing what might be the failure of an entire life to triviality. In the last two stanzas that irony is clearly also directed at himself: it is as though the persona sees how repetitive his own life is, but sees also that he has no choice. **Paradoxically,** although he has accused the characters outside of being 'weak' we are allowed to entertain the possibility that it is the protagonist himself who is weak, unable to take the risk of moving away from his desk, his routine.

But if that is so, says Larkin, then it is a weakness we all share, for it is the common weakness of being unable to face death, and the 'toad work', whatever its deficiencies, at least helps to mark our days and to prevent us from a slow meaningless drift towards obliteration: 'by clouds covered'.

Part four
Critical approaches

Themes

The poetic persona

Larkin's poems seem very often to be in some sense about himself. If we think of 'The Whitsun Weddings', 'High Windows' or the 'Toads' poems, we see thoughts and reflections very close to the surface which impress us as Larkin's own. There is much use of the first-person pronoun ('That Whitsun, I was late getting away', 'At first, I didn't notice', 'Struck, I leant / More promptly out next time'); there are references, such as the ones to the 'in-tray' and the 'loaf-haired secretary' in 'Toads Revisited', which seem very close to Larkin's working life as a librarian.

But the self that Larkin presents to us is a curious one and, like all such poetic **personae**, it is really far more carefully constructed than it may at first glance seem. We might helpfully begin to define Larkin's persona through a series of negations. It is not the intricate, clever, articulate self of much **metaphysical** poetry; nor is it the wildly emotional self of **Romanticism**. Rather, Larkin's is a self which claims to be very much at the mercy of outside forces. Many of his poems – 'Dockery and Son' is a good example – seem to be attempts to realise something, but with very great difficulty: we do not receive only the conclusions but the whole process of reflection, and this reflection can be a very jumpy, occasional matter. Larkin's progression in 'Dockery and Son' from his encounter at his old college to his final general observation on age and death is not a linear one, but is compounded of the seemingly random experiences of his train journey – the 'awful pie', the 'Joining and parting lines', moments when the self may be dreaming, asleep or only half-aware, exposed to forces which it cannot control or even fully understand.

What he seems to be saying is that the self is only very rarely capable of coherent, continuous thoughts. For most of the time we are pushed this way and that by our encounters with the outside world; we are all at the mercy of forces greater than ourselves – one might perhaps be reminded of Prime Minister Harold Macmillan's famously weary comments about the

CRITICAL APPROACHES   THEMES

way in which political plans and strategies are constantly derailed by the unpredictable pressure of 'events' – and to pretend otherwise is merely to deal in abstractions and ideals. In this way, although Larkin appears to be talking about himself, he is seeing himself very much as typical of everybody: life proceeds in jerks, fits and starts, like a stopping train, and his best poems try to recount that experience, which is compounded of pressures, accidents, habits, all of which are stronger than our will.

E VERYDAY LIFE

A second readily identifiable theme is the enormous pressure of contemporary life. Everywhere we are surrounded by messages telling us to do things or not to do things; 'Essential Beauty' is a particularly vivid example of this, with its huge advertising billboards which 'block the ends of streets'. These advertisements represent a world of false values or, better, a world in which there are no values at all because everything is reduced to identical images. In this world we lose our power of discrimination, and human life becomes worthless; the human subject becomes emptied, a kind of vacuum into which false hopes and desires can be projected.

In 'Going, Going', Larkin puts this sense of creeping dehumanisation very clearly when he laments that the countryside 'isn't going to last'. The word 'somehow' in the sixth stanza shows that Larkin is not trying to persuade us that he has a worked-out political position, or even that he can justify his doubt or despair in rational terms. Rather, he is speaking of the doubtful and bewildered feelings which are occasionally common to all of us when we suspect that things in the world around us have got out of control. It is not so much that we are being manipulated; more that nobody retains any sense of the whole of English society, and thus there are no real purposes to be looked for in the world around us. Larkin's poetry does not propound for us some kind of grand conspiracy from which we, as ordinary individuals, are excluded; rather, it suggests that purposes are always in some sense hidden and that the actions we may take in the world will only have unpredictable effects if they have any effects at all. One might, perhaps, be tempted to draw a comparison with the **absurdist** school of literature and especially of drama; but where the absurdists – Eugene Ionesco and Harold Pinter among them – grasp for great symbols by means of which to characterise the instability of modern meaning, Larkin tends rather to allow the absurdity of life to trickle out from his scenarios of everyday disappointment and unfulfilment.

At the same time, Larkin insists, this world around us is the only world there is. There is very little of a transcendental religious sense in Larkin; there is little hope of another world which will redeem or compensate for the shortcomings of this one, and thus we must make the best of what we have. For it would be a mistake to regard Larkin as finally a depressing poet. Indeed, in the poems there is often a strange beauty to be found mysteriously in the most unexpected places – in the habit-influenced world of 'The Whitsun Weddings', for example, where although he appears to be far removed from the world of uncles shouting smut, 'the perms, / The nylon gloves and jewellery-substitutes', nevertheless even these can provoke in him the sense of the spiritual we get in the last lines, when the train slows and he feels 'A sense of falling' that is compared to 'an arrow-shower' and to 'rain'. We may see this as a further pessimism, since this life-giving rain is not, after all, falling on us; yet the pessimism is tempered by a sense that at least happiness might be possible somewhere in the world. Yet happiness is not, by its nature, to be measured simply by one universal standard; we might think here of the strange mood of 'The Card-Players'. Does its final line, 'Rain, wind and fire! The secret, bestial peace!' represent happiness? Contentment? Is there perhaps even a weird kind of exhilaration to be found in abandoning oneself to this 'bestial' life, where there is no thought, no self-consciousness, as Dirk simply 'pours himself some more', Old Prijck 'snores with the gale', an abandonment of the pretensions of humanity before some deeper, more animal life that lurks at the back of our minds and offers us – perhaps – some comfort in a realm far away from the disturbing questionings of the intellect.

Human emotions

Out of the theme of everyday life comes this range of mixed emotions which Larkin so frequently describes for us. There is human affection in his poems, but it is often tempered by impatience and a sense of inadequacy; there is sympathy, as for the women in 'Faith Healing' whose inarticulate need is so great as to affect us all, but it is tempered by a sense of the ridiculous and the absurd. Often alongside all of these feelings there lies a considerable envy of other people, barely concealed in 'Dockery and Son', where Larkin's persona wrestles with a sense of loneliness, of having being forgotten, of only barely experiencing life as it passes him by – like, perhaps, a train at a different platform. This envy is used to **ironical** effect in 'Mr Bleaney', where Larkin imagines the life of the previous inhabitant of his own rented room, conjures up for us the presumed pettiness of his life, but ends with two magnificent stanzas where he muses on whether, after all, Bleaney, whoever he was, perhaps understood his own life better than he, Larkin, does.

However, these verses are, to be sure, problematic. The **syntax** is tangled, it remains difficult to follow the thread of Larkin's argument. Indeed, it is a feature of Larkin's **persona** that he very rarely does seem to *know*: there is often a hesitancy about his conclusions, an uncertainty as to whether he really understands other people's lives, which reflects on the one hand a kind of humility before the mysteries of humanity and yet on the other a sometimes ironic despair at the impossibility of entering into the consciousness of other people. In this sense, we might say that Larkin is constantly and painfully touching on one of the great mysteries of poetry, or of literature in general: namely, the **paradox** of writing necessarily intrusively – about the lives of others while at the same time attempting to remain humble before the complexity of experience.

LONELINESS AND LOSS

Larkin, we might say, is pre-eminently a poet of loneliness and loss. The loneliness is frequently bitter and poignant, as in 'Mr Bleaney'; at other times Larkin is able to make it into a rather painful joke, as when at the end of 'Toads Revisited', in the absence of any other company or solace, he invites the 'old toad' work to be his companion and to 'help' him 'down Cemetery Road' – in other words, to keep him company, at least until the time for death comes. There is loss too in 'Church Going', although at first glance we might pass over it without noticing because the words 'much at a loss' are encapsulated in a commonplace method of phrasing.

Literally, of course, we might say that nothing much is being said here. To be 'at a loss' only means to be bewildered, not to know what to do or how to react or behave; yet one might fairly get the sense that in Larkin's poetry the phrase acquires a new, deeper meaning, in which one's petty everyday experiences of uncertainty become directly linked to what one might call – were it not that the phrase seems over-grandiose in the context of Larkin's deflations of pretension! – a sense of cosmic doubt, a sense that connects us back to all that we might have known 'before the fall', whether one imagines that fall in Christian terms or **psychoanalytic** ones.

The sense of loss, then, is not only of a personal loss; as we have seen, in 'Going, Going' Larkin speaks, very obliquely, of a vanishing world 'beyond the town'. There is nothing overtly cosmic here, rather the references are social and, to an extent, the commonplace stuff of conservative regret in the face of inexplicable change. But the selection of the negative word 'louts' is highly deliberate: one of the most complicated things to grasp about Larkin is the way in which, despite the overriding sense of loss in his poetry, he almost never falls fully into nostalgia or pastoral (as one can see particularly in 'Here'). There are exceptions, such as, for instance, 'Cut Grass', which is a short and very beautiful pastoral poem; but in the main Larkin never seems quite sure that even the world that is vanishing would necessarily have been much better than this one. In any case, he might well say, what is the point of wondering about that? That world is 'going' – as, of course, also in the pun in the title of 'Church Going' – and all we can do is make the best of the one which seems already to have taken its place – the world of fast profits, free sex and the rule of commerce, the world through, or down, which we are all sliding without the means to help ourselves.

Death

The new world conveyed by Larkin does not have the final word itself, although it may think it has, because in the end all this new world is trying to do is to cover over the deep unchanging facts of sickness and death, and ultimately it is in his dealings with these inexorable realities that Larkin often seems at his most powerful. The first stanza of 'Ambulances' is typical of this side of Larkin's poetry. The image of the 'confessionals' is important; for Larkin often appears to be saying that although death is the end of all things and frequently terrible, nevertheless there is a sense in which we all yearn towards it, towards its privacy, its utter relevance to our *selves*, as though our death is the one thing we can incontrovertibly call our own, the place where we can at last come face to face with something which is true and which is protected from the debasements of the world outside. Beside this sense of peace, the 'Loud noons of cities' fall back into their proper triviality; the ambulances and all they represent are far stronger than any other force and can afford to ignore the 'glances', and yet they are also intensely commonplace, and sickness and death are all around us, 'at any kerb'. In this image the matter-of-factness of ambulances as road vehicles and their symbolic stature as harbingers of the end of all things are marvellously conjured.

To pursue this further might take us back again to that strange poem, 'Nothing To Be Said', and particularly to the uses Larkin there makes of the phrase 'slow dying'. Perhaps life is indeed 'slow dying', as he says in the first stanza; but then again, maybe this is better than other sorts of dying, and even the 'nations vague as weed' gain some kind of stature from their relics, their remains. For the fact of the matter, as Larkin himself says, is that one view of the purpose of writing – his own view, as he expresses it – is to 'preserve experience', and so there is an implicit **paradox** in writing about 'going', about vanishing, about the disappearance of the humane, for the very act of writing about it in some sense preserves it, ensures that the experience is not entirely consigned to the crypt of history but remains alive, or at least capable of being re-enlivened as we read. It may seem an over-obvious thing to say, but it is surely true that if Larkin-the-man felt as pessimistic as Larkin-the-**persona** often seems to do, then he would not have been writing poems in the first place, and we as readers would not be sharing in this complex set of explorations of hope and despair, life and death, survival and disappearance.

Maybe, then, the last line on Larkin's themes should be the last line of 'The Explosion': 'One showing the eggs unbroken'. Here, it seems – as throughout this marvellous poem – there is a perfectly conjured sense of all that amazingly survives the wreck of life, the dissolution of hope. Perhaps it is too much to hope – Larkin might say – that many of us will manage to carry life's eggs unbroken – or to carry them at all or, indeed, to find them in the first place – but nevertheless, here is an example of an overwhelming sense of hope overcoming all negative evidence, and if that triumph is only a matter of fantasy, then perhaps this does not matter: perhaps it is only in the realm of fantasy – or the imagination – that such triumphs can occur, and in any case it is through these fantasies, these imaginative leaps and identifications, that we live our lives in the first place. There would of course have been to the romantic poets, for example, an enormous difference between fantasy and imagination; but in Larkin we may fairly say that this is not the important difference. What is important is the difference between imaginings that help us to manage our lives against the omnipresent presence of death, and those other imposed fantasies at the service of society in general which, while they appear to promise a better life through, for example, commerce or religious belief, in fact merely deplete us and render us empty subjects.

Language and style

Poetic form

In his mature poems Larkin uses a variety of forms, but we can list a number of features which link his best work together. First, these forms are all quite regular: Larkin is not much interested in free verse, and it is largely in this respect that we can see the influences he received from nineteenth-century poetry and from the tradition of Hardy. He seems not so much rejective of **modernism** as oblivious to it.

All of his major poems rhyme, and very often Larkin manages to make this rhyming unobtrusive by relying on quite small, unimportant words, and by using a good deal of half-rhyme. Consider, for example, the rhyming words in the first two stanzas of 'The Building': 'hotel', 'see', 'fall', 'century', 'up', 'hall', 'smell', 'cup', 'sit', 'mags', 'bus', 'bags', 'although', 'nurse' – none of these are uncommon words, or words which carry much resonance in themselves.

If, however, we look more closely at 'The Building', we can also see the intricacy of the way in which Larkin builds his rhyme-schemes, for the poem consists of nine seven-line stanzas, plus a final separated line – sixty-four lines in all – whereas the rhyme scheme operates on an *eight*-line scheme of ABCBDCAD. This makes the rhyming less apparent; it acts as a device to carry us unconsciously on from one stanza to the next; it also builds up the isolation and ambiguity of the separated final line, 'With wasteful, weak, propitiatory flowers', for by the end of the ninth stanza we have a sense that we need this final line to make formal sense of the poem as a whole.

This complicated stanza form is again typical of Larkin's poetry as a whole. He uses lines containing four or five stressed syllables – tetrameters and pentameters – and often stanzas of between four and eight lines, but very few poems are exactly the same. Consider again, for example, 'The Whitsun Weddings', where the run of pentameters is interrupted in each stanza by a second line of two stressed syllables. This is not an accidental feature: this sudden break in each stanza almost before it has begun comes to represent the hesitant movement of a train, which sometimes seems to stop arbitrarily – not in a station, or at the end of a stanza, but in the middle of nowhere.

For a very different example of Larkin's formal mastery, we can look at one of his very few free verse poems, 'Days'. Here there is no rhyme and the lines are all short and appear to conform to no particular syllabic structure. But the poem is held together by certain words – 'days' repeated three times; 'they' also repeated three times (and, of course, an almost-rhyme with 'days'); the 'v' sounds of 'live', 'over', 'live' again, 'solving', 'over' again. This poem also gains a strong effect precisely from the breakage of form: from the sense that the last four lines do not really fit with the first six. This is itself a deliberate representation of the way in which these doctors and priests, who are supposed traditionally to bring answers or at least cures to the problems of life, in fact only compound our sense of life's mystery.

But 'Days' is unusual; for the most part, Larkin writes in large, stately, capacious stanzas, and his best poems are probably those in pentameter form – which is the major form of traditional English versification, the preferred form of, for example, Shakespeare and Wordsworth. This line length allows Larkin room to expand his thoughts; but it also allows him to introduce a dialectic, an argument, between the debasement of contemporary life which is so frequently his theme and something grander, larger, more stable.

Thus Larkin's use of form becomes in itself part of the argument he is trying to conduct. It stands as a statement that there is a value in tradition: not a value we all have to accept unthinkingly but one which can be recurringly demonstrated in the practice of poetry itself. From the discussion of the themes in Larkin's poetry above, it might seem as though his ideas on the contemporary decline of civilisation are similar to those of T. S. Eliot, and to an extent they are; but whereas in Eliot these ideas need to be replicated in a breaking down of traditional forms, Larkin sees such forms as a counterbalance to the surrounding decay. This is not, however, a point he wishes to force upon us; rather he wants it to become clear as we muse on the forms of his verse. We may observe the way in which he is able to talk about, for example, despair *at the same time as* rendering that feeling into well-formed poetry.

The main issue here, however, is to notice the interplay between the traditional forms and the actual uses of language which Larkin deploys. If we look again at the opening of 'Going, Going', we can see something of this: 'I thought it would last my time – / The sense that, beyond the town'. These are perfectly formed lines, trimeters in fact, but there is a jauntiness to their rhythm which undercuts any possible sense of formality. Larkin is a master of the art of matching formal versification with the rhythms of everyday speech – in these two opening lines there is nothing which could not occur in an ordinary conversation. We can turn again to the opening stanza of 'Dockery and Son' to follow through this point in greater detail. This stanza, like almost all the poem, is written in pentameters, but we notice immediately the break of rhythm in the very first line, the effect of which is to reinforce the casualness of this opening conversation (the rhythm is broken only once more, very near the end of the poem). Within these pentameters, however, Larkin is able to convey an astonishing variety of discourses. There is the casual conversation with the Dean. There is the internal description of 'Death-suited, visitant, I nod'. There is the reflective memory. There is the colloquialism of 'half-tight'. There is the reported, formulaic speech of 'our version' and 'these incidents last night'. Larkin is able to make all of these fragments into an intricate weave, held together by a solid rhythm; perhaps here we see something of the connection between his poetry and his lifelong interest in jazz, where the combination of consistent rhythm and the free interplay of different instruments is all-important.

Larkin's poetry is noted for its colloquialisms, although in fact there are quite few. In the main, what we find in the poetry is a determined attempt to represent ordinary speech and the common processes of thought and feeling. This comes out very strongly in an extraordinary unfinished poem called 'The Dance', in which Larkin recounts an encounter at a dance in complicated eleven-line stanzas. The poem includes these lines:

> I face you on the floor, clumsily, as
> Something starts up. Your look is challenging
> And not especially friendly: everything
> I look to for protection – the mock jazz,
> The gilt-edged Founder, through the door
> The 'running buffet supper' – grows less real.
> Suddenly it strikes me you are acting more
> Than ever you would put into words; I feel
> The impact, open, raw,
> Of a tremendous answer banging back
>
> As if I'd asked a question. In the slug
> And snarl of music, under cover of
> A few permitted movements, you suggest
> A whole consenting language, that my chest
> Quickens and tightens at, descrying love …

Notice first the movement of the very first line, where the notion of clumsiness is so brilliantly underlined by the clumsiness of the line itself, ending as if by accident with the hanging 'as'. Again, the word 'something' suggests a **colloquial** vagueness, as though Larkin is trying not to dress an experience up in poetic terms thought of later but to recount how the experience was at the time, with all its gaps and uncertainties.

The 'running buffet supper' is of course a colloquial phrase, and one here rendered absurd by its contrast with what is happening to the narrator of this story. When we come to the word 'banging', we sense something quite frequent in Larkin: the way in which he is content to use words which may seem at first glance colloquially inaccurate rather than search for more acceptable equivalents. The point, however, is that by the use of this term, and the 'slug' and 'snarl' of the music, he creates a far more vivid sense of the occasion – itself rather cheap and conducive to cheapened emotions – than could be done otherwise. Larkin does not mean to beautify or idealise the experience but to represent, to 'preserve' it, as it was.

No poem, of course, can simply 'preserve' an experience, because the very act of writing and forming implies some kind of change; but another of Larkin's strengths is that, as well as wishing to signal the immediacy of his experience, he is often simultaneously able to indicate his inner distance from it; and he does so here in his use of the word 'descrying', which is fascinating in this context for two reasons. On the one hand, the word means 'to see from a vast distance' and thus signifies a division in Larkin's persona here between the man who is involved in the dance and the man who is compulsively observing it from the outside; on the other, 'descrying' is also a slightly **archaic**, erudite term which conjures the whole area of the persona's reserved, scholarly being, which cannot become fully involved in this arena of seduction.

Thus Larkin's use of form and style often serves to join different realms of experience, in particular this difficult area between the poet's humanity and his being a poet. It is one of Larkin's major strengths that, as he always wanted to be, he became a poet capable of speaking to an audience to whom these ordinary feelings are familiar without thereby sacrificing the enormous skill and craft he had at his disposal.

IMAGERY AND SYMBOLISM

The difference between an **image** and a **symbol** is a puzzling one, and has been explained in many different ways. Principally, it is a question of force. We use imagery all the time: we talk, for example, of someone having a sunny disposition, and we do not mean that literally: we are implicitly comparing the person's temperament to the sun, and in a specific way – we are thinking of the sun as signifying cheerfulness, light rather than dark, warmth rather than cold. At the same time we are necessarily ignoring other attributes of the sun: we do not mean, for example, that the person would make you go blind if you looked steadily at him or her, nor do we mean that the person is millions of miles away from us.

Thus imagery implies selection; and to a large extent that selection is for us to make. Just so with poetry, a poet will select an image for his or her own purposes. A symbol is a more considerable matter: to refer directly to the sun, or to the moon as Larkin does in 'Dockery and Son', or to a lion or an eagle, is to call upon an already existing range of associations which we can tamper with and use but which are not our property as individuals. We cannot make a lion into a symbol of weakness no matter how hard we try: the cowardly lion in *The Wizard of Oz* is indeed a joke about how far we can alter the limits of symbolism.

But in poetry strange things can, and do, happen. Some of the images which poets coin, because of the sheer strength of the language in which they are expressed, attain a kind of symbolic force: they may have a clear purpose, but they also have a halo of mystery which can never be fully explained. The question of whether Larkin was or was not a symbolic poet is one which has occupied many critics, but it need not worry us here; suffice to say that he was a poet who, like every other poet, used imagery, and sometimes that imagery carried a symbolic force. Here we shall look at four of the most startling images in his poetry and try to see through these images towards the themes already discussed.

These four images are: (a) the image of the toads in 'Toads' and 'Toads Revisited'; (b) the image of the couple in 'An Arundel Tomb'; (c) the image of the arrow-shower in 'The Whitsun Weddings'; (d) the image of the high windows in the poem of that name. We have already talked briefly about all of these images in the Commentaries section above.

The toads, for Larkin, signify ugliness, weight, something which is immovable, and something which continues to exist whether we want it to or not. The very way a real toad sits suggests something which cannot be shifted, something which leads a very different life from our own and which cannot be ignored. This, of course, is what Larkin is saying about what he calls 'work': but by 'work' he means something broader – the whole burden of habit and routine which exerts power over us. The toads thus signify a limit upon choice. We may think that we choose what kind of life to lead, we may imagine we are in control of decisions about our own life, career, relationships, but the toads remind us that we are really at the mercy of forces that we do not totally understand. While we think we are controlling everyday life, it is in fact everyday life that is controlling us. The toad's purposes are, to us, inscrutable, unintelligible; in the same way, the patterns which our lives take cannot be fully comprehended by us. Life is something which happens to us, whether we want it to or not.

The image of the couple on the tomb makes a convergent point, although from a very different perspective. What Larkin is saying there is that the real couple whose memorial the tomb is could have had little idea of the future; they might not have known exactly how they were to be commemorated in stone, but more importantly they could not even have guessed whether or how their memorial would survive, still less what people of future generations would come to make of it.

The connection between the 'Toads' poems and 'An Arundel Tomb' is that we are again seeing an image of the lack of real control we have over our own lives, and even over our deaths and what might happen to our names and our reputations after we are gone. The difference is that whereas the toads signify a kind of brute ugliness, the image of the couple is, at least from one angle, a thing of beauty. What Larkin is therefore saying is that even art – here the art of the sculptor, but by implication also the art of the writer, of the poet – signifies an aspect of the lack of control the individual really exerts over his or her own life.

The arrow-shower in 'The Whitsun Weddings' relates closely to these images. We cannot know, Larkin says, where this arrow-shower will land; in other words, we cannot know what effect our lives and our perceptions will have on other people. This is similar, again, to the issue of poetry: a poet may write with one thing in mind, but when his or her text is read it might be that it produces effects which are quite different. In the case of 'The Whitsun Weddings', it seems also as though he is saying something more than this. The weddings themselves, as he portrays them, are not events with a great deal of intrinsic beauty: they are ritualised, formalised; the people who participate in them do not possess much of what is generally regarded as good taste. Nevertheless, in the mind of the persona of the poem, and for reasons which he cannot fully explain, they seem to represent a sort of hope.

This reflects something which matters greatly to Larkin, which is that if we cannot find some echo of beauty among the common rituals and forms of our culture, then we cannot find it anywhere. Even the toads have something to reveal, but what is revealed by the toads, by the Arundel couple, by the arrow-shower, is that we can find hope and beauty only by relinquishing our perpetual anxious wish to be in control of our own destiny. We must realise and even embrace the limitations which are ours because we are human; we must not look to a more perfect, a more ordered or a less fearful world to save us from the present one, but instead we must learn to live in the present with all the tolerance of imperfection and muddle which such living demands.

Thus Larkin's own imagery reflects something of what was said above: namely that the image which attains to symbolic force does so only by accepting that there is something mysterious and inexplicable which we have to tolerate and live with, even if this means that we also have an ever-present sense of disappointment. Much of Larkin's imagery, then, relates to ways of living with this disappointment: not exulting in it, nor trying to sweep it under the carpet, but accepting it as part of the texture of our everyday lives.

We can connect the 'high windows' with this body of imagery, for the high windows simultaneously represent the imagining of a better, freer life and the impossibility of breaking through the 'window' to inhabit this better life – except, perhaps, at the moment of death. The high windows are mysterious: does our occasional awareness of freedom relieve us from the tedium of our everyday lot, or does it throw our existence into a terrible relief and reinforce our discontent? Larkin does not answer this question, and his refusal to answer it is enormously important. Poetry is poetry and not another thing because it does not answer questions, because it recognises that at a very deep level the most serious questions are not answerable.

The image, then, or the symbol, stands in place of an answer. At the deeper levels of our personalities, in those realms which are revealed in dreams, we do not find answers, nor do we find clearly defined categories or oppositions. We all know the experience when we have, for example, dreamed of a beast and have woken up remembering it as, for example, a lion. But when we come to try to describe it to somebody, we realise that in fact it had wings, our mother's eyes, and it spoke to us. The beast of which we dreamed was not clearly one thing or another: it was compounded of bits and pieces; it included contradictions in its make-up.

This is the case with poetry, and particularly with poetic imagery; and this, of course, is the basis of the reason why the study of poetry is not easy. It is not easy for us to understand or to live with images which seem contradictory, as do the arrow-shower and the high windows; but this is also precisely why poetry is so important, because it shows us a world within us where easy answers are not to be found. It demands not our acquiescence, our agreement, but our imaginative participation.

PART FIVE

Background

The life of Philip Larkin

Philip Larkin was born in Coventry in 1922, and went to the King Henry VIII School there, where, by his own account, he was good at nothing but English, and spent most of his time reading. He went to the University of Oxford in 1940, and there we have evidence of his second major interest aside from poetry: jazz, about which he wrote some memorable pieces of criticism. Among his friends at Oxford were Kingsley Amis and John Wain, both of whom were to exert a strong influence on his early writing. He achieved a first-class degree in 1943, but had no clear idea of a career.

He drifted into a job as librarian at the public library in Wellington, and it was while he was there, in 1945, that he produced his first volume of poetry, *The North Ship*. His influences then clearly included W.B. Yeats and Dylan Thomas. Although *The North Ship* included some good poems, and even more good phrases, it gave little hint as to where his poetry was to take him. In 1946 he published a novel, *Jill*, which was to a considerable extent based on his experiences in war-time Oxford; and this was followed in 1947 by a second novel, *A Girl in Winter*.

By this time Larkin was working in the library at the University of Leicester, where he remained until 1950, when he moved to a similar but superior job at Queen's University, Belfast. It was at this point in the early 1950s that he began to develop the poetic style which we now associate with him; and these were, by Larkin's standards, prolific years, culminating in 1955 in the publication of the collection *The Less Deceived*. Some of his work was also included in two very important anthologies of the period, *Poets of the 1950s* edited by D.J. Enright in 1950, and *New Lines*, edited by Robert Conquest in 1956.

The Less Deceived was a considerable success, and was reprinted three times during the year after its first publication. At this time, Larkin moved from Northern Ireland to take the position of librarian at the university library at Hull, a position which he held until his death. His third volume of poems, *The Whitsun Weddings*, was published in 1964, and consolidated his reputation as one of Britain's foremost poets; he was awarded the Queen's

Gold Medal for Poetry in 1965. His fourth and final volume, *High Windows*, appeared in 1974. On the death of the then poet laureate, Sir John Betjeman, in 1984 it was widely rumoured that Larkin would be his successor; and although the reasons why he was not have not been made fully public, it seems likely that ill-health and a lifelong habit of seclusion were partly responsible. Certainly by that time – and his death followed one year later – he was Britain's best-known poet, and one of the most quoted.

Larkin's life was, after all, extraordinary in the most obvious ways: he was a lifelong bachelor, and a man apparently wary of deep personal relationships. In a lesser poet this might well have limited his field of human sympathy; it is a remarkable feature of Larkin's writing that he is able to deploy his outsider status wittily, **ironically**, and to the advantage of his reader as he ceaselessly compared his own situation with the situations of those he sees around him.

In one of the most splendid of his poems, 'An Arundel Tomb', Larkin describes the dignity of death, but is unable to prevent himself from mentioning a 'faint hint of the absurd' in the whole business of surviving, in any form, after one has gone. This sense of the necessity of preservation, combined with the ridiculousness of assigning to any individual life more than is its due, is intrinsic to his poetry; and so perhaps Larkin himself had more to say on the nature of biography than any future commentator can ever have.

Historical & Literary Background

The Movement

The anthologies in which Larkin was published in the 1950s amounted to a manifesto for a group of British poets known simply as 'The Movement', and Larkin's work was seen as central to this poetic tendency. Basically, the Movement formed its ideas in reaction to previous movements in British poetry. Where T. S. Eliot and the **modernists** of the 1920s had preached the value of difficulty and had opened themselves to new influences from past traditions in English literature and from European and American writing, the Movement stood for simplicity and even **colloquialism** of expression and adopted firmly British – or perhaps English – values and forms. Where W. H. Auden and the political poets of the 1930s exalted the social role of the poet and the necessity of political change, the Movement returned to the everyday and to a poetry firmly divorced from political programmes. Where Dylan Thomas and the 'New Apocalyptics' of the 1940s spoke of the intensity of their emotions and practised in consequence a dislocation of ordinary syntax, the Movement prided itself on keeping the emotions under firm control and tended to regard poetry as one part of the everyday communication of one person to others.

The Movement was concerned with economy of expression and with tightness of verse form; and these are very much skills in tune with Larkin's genius. Although he chose to make very few public pronouncements on his writing, most of them concentrated on the need for a poetry which moves beyond an 'initiated' audience and can find some kind of resonance with common experience. There is a certain irony here, since by far the majority of Movement poets were academics and many of them were, or became, substantial critics in their own right. However, the Movement still stood for a separation of poetic and academic activity, and laid claim to a broad audience, a claim which, not surprisingly, it found it hard to acquit.

Ted Hughes

Much can be gained by comparing Larkin's poetic environment and development with that of his nearest rival to poetic fame over the last forty years, Ted Hughes, who was appointed to the laureateship in 1984. Hughes was a poet of the vast distances; most of his poetry is set in rural surroundings, or in the grinding daily life of people who are themselves remote from society. Larkin always preferred to look at more common lives, lives in suburbia, lives in small towns. Where Hughes tended to look for transcendental meanings and to find these by contrasting the inadequacies of human life with the instinctual harmonies of the animal kingdom, Larkin remained content to extract meanings painstakingly from the rituals and ceremonies with which we attempt to surround and protect lives which might otherwise be thoroughly debased.

Angry Young Men

As we read through Larkin's poetry we can sense some of the movements of contemporary history. His first novel, *Jill*, has often been compared with the novels of the 'Angry Young Men' – John Braine, Alan Sillitoe and others – and while this is not a very happy comparison it is true that Larkin transparently belongs to a generation who hoped for much after the Second World War, and were disappointed.

But disappointment did not make Larkin angry; or rather, anger is not one of the moods most frequently reflected in his poetry. It contributes rather to a strong but gentle **irony**: a sense that any ideal exists only to be betrayed, and therefore perhaps it is better not to have ideals at all. But even that makes Larkin's poetry sound too prescriptive: for Larkin does not try to teach us how to live, rather he shows us some of the accommodations he has made with the problems of living and some of the accommodations other people make, and invites his readers to inspect them.

Britain in the 1960s and beyond

British society, of course, went through a major upheaval in the 1960s. The painful austerity of the immediate post-war years – made all the more painful by the contemporary hopes for a rapid transformation and opening-up of a stagnant society, hopes which although not entirely dashed were never met in full measure – gave way to a sudden affluence, and a sense that therefore many of the restrictions of an older way of life were no longer necessary. These were the years of the 'generation gap', years when the young went into wholesale revolt against received wisdom; and in several of his poems of the period Larkin reflects ruefully on the attraction of this sense of coming freedom and hope, although always from the position of a man already too old and too set in his ways fully to benefit from it.

As time has passed, the sense of imminent change that prevailed throughout the 1960s has been increasingly replaced by a new awareness of constraint: the real economic constraint which must operate in a country which is no longer as powerful as it once was, and the wider constraint to do with how we can manage with a world of diminishing resources. It seems fair to say that, as British society has turned full circle back to the rigours of a rationed economy – even if not as literally rationed as in the 1950s – we have, so to speak, Larkin waiting for us. For he was never carried away on the wave of optimism; there remained throughout his poetry a sense that any success, any achievement, has to be paid for, especially in a society in which freedom is less natural than an unthinking obedience to the power of tradition.

His poetry actually displays a very strong sense of the generations: of siblings, of fathers and sons, of the intricacies of the family. Often the family does serve as a site for claustrophobia: yet in a Larkin poem we can rarely be free from ambiguities in this area, as Larkin on the one hand appears to relish his freedom from ties while on the other suggesting the real human warmth which the family can (if only occasionally) provide. The emotions which Larkin seems to wish to conjure up are always *tempered* ones: satisfaction shadowed by regret, mournfulness edged with hope, despair about communication tinged with a curious elation about being free.

LITERARY INFLUENCES

Isolating the literary influences at work on Larkin's poetry is not simple. Clearly the early influences of **symbolism**, through Yeats and Thomas, waned, although they never disappeared entirely. Whether Larkin was ever *influenced* by the Movement (see section on The Movement above) is harder to say; perhaps the best way of putting it is that the Movement was a group of people working under similar influences, which induced in them a particular kind of realism in their attitudes to life as well as to poetry. We might then fairly say that Larkin stayed within that ambit throughout his writing life, and certainly **modernist** and **post-modernist** developments in literature had little visible effect on his style.

The great influence claimed by the Movement was the poetry of Thomas Hardy, and here one can see a useful comparison, for Larkin was always concerned with the traditional rhythms of English poetry, with the everyday scenes and sights of English life. But all of this seems less than conscious in Larkin: less as though he is making a choice than as though his thoughts are naturally attuned to the standard English verse-forms.

Also, Larkin's poetry is much more clearly acerbic than Hardy's, and can be very terse indeed. In a good number of his poems he seems deliberately to disown elegance and accuracy of language and to opt instead for the debased language of contemporary usage. He is famous, for example, for his use of swear words. But in this he is not totally at odds with Hardy, because, of course, the occasionally scurrilous tone of Larkin's language might be considered as parallel to Hardy's usage of the social decencies of his own time.

We might suggest that Larkin's life had a shape which was eccentric – in his singleness, in his job, in his improbable background for a poet – and yet emblematic, insofar as he shared many of the frustrations and difficulties of people of his generation; and it is this conjunction of marginality and common understanding which lies behind the greatness of his poetry – as, perhaps, it lay behind Shakespeare's.

PART SIX

CRITICAL HISTORY AND FURTHER READING

CONTEMPORARY CRITICISM

Larkin's poetry has sparked a great deal of controversy in recent years, although of a rather unusual kind. We can begin to understand something of this controversy by noticing that during his lifetime, or rather during the time when he was writing and publishing his major poetry, he was frequently seen as a 'confessional' poet. In other words, it was supposed that the views put forward in the poems, the positions espoused, the moods conjured up, could be directly linked to Larkin's own views, positions and moods.

The very notion of 'confessional poetry' is, however, inherently problematic. It supposes, firstly, that one can read directly back from the poem to the author and, secondly, that it is possible for the author to manifest his intentions directly in his work. Both of these ideas have been repeatedly challenged by recent critical theory, especially by the **post-structuralist** school operating in the wake of Roland Barthes' influential essay, 'The Death of the Author', which suggests that the author is forever inaccessible and that any attempt to interrogate the author through the text is only a version of the pathetic fallacy. According to this theory, the author is in no sense present in his or her work; the words are independent of their author and, in the famous formulation of Jacques Derrida, 'there is nothing outside the text'.

Reading Larkin in this 'confessional' fashion, however, did encourage a certain set of social and political assumptions. Larkin was, it was proposed, a lower-middle-class author, and his perceptions and preoccupations, even when heavily ironised, were of that class and associated with a particular kind of background, upbringing, perspective. This could be seen positively, in the sense that Larkin could be taken to be speaking for a certain version of 'middle England' and to be an 'authentic' voice rather than one trammelled by the requirements of 'high literature'; or it could be seen negatively, in that the prejudices and **stereotypes** which abound in his poetry could be seen as limitations on his judgement and moral generosity.

For the most part, while Larkin was alive critical opinion on these matters tended towards the positive. Larkin's undoubted and unchallenged skills in the making of striking verse were regarded as in the service of a vision which, although it was usually ironic, sometimes caustic, often despairing, was nonetheless central to an 'English' sensibility, and in this sense Larkin spoke to and for a large and broad audience, almost as though he was the poetic or cultural equivalent of the Church of England. It was for these reasons that it was so widely assumed that he would become Poet Laureate, and that there was considerable surprise when it was gathered that he had turned the post down. According to this reading Larkin's poetry might seem occasionally churlish and curmudgeonly, but it was essentially an accepting and forgiving poetry which, even when it talks of those who are 'Moustached in flowered frocks', is only gently mocking the vast variety of human nature.

Posthumous criticism

During the years following his death, a profound shock occurred. Many of Larkin's letters were discovered, and a selection of them was published, edited by Anthony Thwaite, also the editor of his *Collected Poems*, in 1992. It transpired that Larkin's letters – some of which constituted a lengthy epistolary relationship with the novelist, cynic and renowned curmudgeon Kingsley Amis – showed a side of Larkin which, although it appears in muted form in the poetry, disturbed many critics and readers. They showed him as deeply misogynistic; as an ingrained and unashamed racist; and as a man in whom a vein of self-pity ran far too deep for any kind of comfort. Obviously, for a critical tradition which regarded the boundary between the writing and the writer as permeable, this posed a problem of major difficulty: how could one go on revering the poetry of a person of such appalling moral prejudice, a person who appeared from the evidence of the letters to lack any sense of sympathy with others and to revel in scorn and contempt?

It would be fair to say that Larkin's reputation has not fully recovered from these revelations; indeed, it is possible that it never will. Not only were the 'confessional critics' deeply troubled; more politically correct schools of criticism, including **feminists**, excoriated Larkin and there were demands that his poetry be removed from school and academic syllabuses.

Yet in a way, it seems fair to say that this monster was of the critics' own making; for if one were to adopt a different critical position, then the question of Larkin's own opinions would be of less, if any, importance. The probable violence of Christopher Marlowe; the appalling sexual attitudes of the **Restoration** writers; the undoubted drunkenness of writers as diverse as William Faulkner, Dylan Thomas and Brendan Behan; the fascist flirtations of Ezra Pound: none of these have substantially dented the reputation of the writer, or at least not to the extent that has occurred, at least for the moment, in Larkin's case. This is in part due to the nature of the offence given; in part to cultural changes which have rendered more things impermissible than may have been the case in the past; but also in part, it would appear, to a certain disappointment, as though the 'exposure' of Larkin was also an unwelcome exposure of the dark side of that 'middle England' for which he had been supposed to speak.

The student will, unfortunately, not find any substantial criticism which takes a different view; most of the existing criticism, while respecting Larkin's technical virtuosity, reflects one side or the other of the debate outlined above. To move further in critical apprehension, it would be necessary to move away from a concern with Larkin as person and to look more deeply at the poetry and at its major themes, and here, oddly enough, one can find that, the poetry has far more in common with the major poststructuralist emphases than might appear at first glance.

Poststructuralist criticism

If we were to take this approach, then the first thing we might say is that essentially Larkin's poetry is a poetry which is concerned, as is all **poststructural** criticism, with the nature of desire. There is a desire for community, a wish to be part of something greater than the lonely individual self. There is also, as for example in 'High Windows', a desire for the transcendental, for some possibility of moving beyond the mundane; but alongside this there is also a knowledge that such transcendence is not fully possible, that the soul is bound to the body and to the dull round of repetition. There is, as for example in 'Talking in Bed', a desire for intimacy, a desire to know and to be known by the 'other'; with, at the same time, a despondent awareness of the impossibility of full communication.

Alongside this, one may see Larkin's poetry as characterised by a continual preoccupation with mortality and death. One senses that many of the poems represent moments snatched from the jaws of death, but all too frequently they end with the black ship towing a 'huge and birdless silence', a vision of death in which all lives and all words are drowned. Beyond this there is the depressive's terrible awareness that if death is all there is to come, then there is no real value to be assigned to our efforts in the here and now; all will be wiped out – has already, as it were, been wiped out – by the inexorable approach of annihilation. This sense of impermanence, of the transitory nature of writing and of the human capacity for self-delusion in the face of the inevitable, is again a major poststructuralist theme.

For the 'confessional critics', for those who believe in the inseparability of biography and fiction, there is a single unitary self or 'subject' to which all things can be referred and against which all things can be measured. For the poststructuralist, subjectivity is dispersed and scattered, as it is in, for example, the multiple hesitations of 'Dockery and Son', a question of 'Joining and parting lines'. Not only is it dispersed and scattered; it is not even under our own control. We are – as we are in, for example, 'Essential Beauty' – at the mercy of forces more powerful than ourselves, forces against which we cannot fight because they have already played a large part in the formation of our personalities and the structuring of our desires. There is, then, for the poststructuralist no possibility of real unity, only of a mourning for a unity which is forever lost; just so Larkin repeatedly bemoans the impossibility of arriving at a full, assured self, and even the apparently assured endings of many of his major poems have a certain temporary, provisional quality to them.

'Mr Bleaney' is one of the best examples of this. The poem seems to express a yearning to live one's life, as it were, within oneself; but instead we are constantly forced into a mould by society. Even when – or perhaps especially when – we think we are most 'ourselves', we have no real self to be; we are rather the effect of those who have gone before us (as in 'This Be The Verse') or, like the new tenant in 'Mr Bleaney', we find ourselves constructing ourselves only in the light of others – from, indeed, the debris of others – and trying to imagine what it would be like to be an other as a substitute for a kind of hollowing out of the self.

It is in no way a negative criticism of Larkin's poetry to say that it is, in the end, a poetry of emptiness and hollowness. At the heart of the poems we may often sense a vacuum, an abyss, as inhuman and separated as the inside of an ambulance, into which we dread we might tumble. The poems themselves we might see as mechanisms to prevent, or postpone, this always imminent collapse. Their assured rhythms, their convoluted and brilliant rhymes, their technical mastery, their syntactical elegance, all these appear dedicated to the task of building something solid and durable; yet, as Larkin's own reputation has already shown, with the utmost irony, perhaps this solidity, this durability is in the end unavailable – either to human beings or indeed to writing.

Further reading

Works by Philip Larkin:

> *The North Ship*, Fortune Press, 1945
>
> *Jill*, Fortune Press, 1946
>
> *A Girl in Winter*, Faber and Faber, 1947
>
> *The Less Deceived*, The Marvell Press, 1955
>
> *The Whitsun Weddings*, Faber and Faber, 1964
>
> *All What Jazz: A Record Diary 1961–68*, Faber and Faber, 1970
>
> *High Windows*, Faber and Faber, 1971
>
> *Required Writing: Miscellaneous Pieces 1955–82*, Faber and Faber, 1983
>
> *Collected Poems*, ed. Anthony Thwaite, The Marvell Press and Faber and Faber, 1988
>
> *Selected Letters of Philip Larkin, 1940–1985*, ed. Anthony Thwaite, Faber and Faber, 1992
>
> *Further Requirements: Interviews, Broadcasts, Statements and Reviews, 1952–1985*, ed. Anthony Thwaite, Faber and Faber, 2001

Books on Philip Larkin:

Alan Brownjohn, *Philip Larkin*, Writers and their Work Series, Longman for the British Council, 1975 (now out of print)

Linda Cookson and Bryan Loughrey, eds, *Critical Essays on Philip Larkin: The Poems*, Longman, 1989 (now out of print)

Roger Day, *Larkin*, Open University Press, 1987 (now out of print)

George Hartley, ed., *Philip Larkin 1922–85: A Tribute*, Marvell Press, 1988

Laurence Lerner, *Philip Larkin*, Plymouth Northcote House Educational Publishers, 1997

Bruce K. Martin, *Philip Larkin*, Twayne University Press, 1978 (now out of print)

Andrew Motion, *Philip Larkin*, Faber and Faber, 1994

Stephen Regan, ed., *Philip Larkin*, Palgrave Macmillan, 1997

Janice Rossen, *Philip Larkin: His Life's Work*, University of Iowa Press, 1990

Dale Salwak, ed., *Philip Larkin: The Man and his Work*, University of Iowa Press, 1989 (now out of print)

David Timms, *Philip Larkin*, Oliver and Boyd, 1973 (now out of print)

CHRONOLOGY

World events	Author's life	Literary events
	1922 Born in Coventry	
		1934 Robert Graves, *I, Claudius*; T. S. Eliot, *The Rock*
		1935 T. S. Eliot, *Murder in the Cathedral*
1936 Accession of Edward VIII; abdication of Edward VIII and accession of George VI; Jarrow to London march; start of Spanish Civil War		
1937 Neville Chamberlain becomes British Prime Minister		**1937** George Orwell, *The Road to Wigan Pier*
1939–45 Second World War		**1939** James Joyce, *Finnegans Wake*
1940 Winston Churchill becomes Prime Minister	**1940–43** Attends the University of Oxford	
	1943 Begins work at a library in Wellington	
1945 Clement Atlee becomes British Prime Minister	**1945** First volume of poetry, *The North Ship*	**1945** Evelyn Waugh, *Brideshead Revisited*; George Orwell, *Animal Farm*; Philip Larkin, *The North Ship*; J. B. Priestley, *An Inspector calls*
	1946 First novel, *Jill*; Becomes Assistant Librarian at the University of Leicester	
1946 National Insurance Act establishes comprehensive insurance system based on Beveridge scheme; National Health Act provides free health care to all; Bank of England and coal industry nationalised; Cold War begins		
1947 Economic crisis in Britain; USA offers Marshall Aid to Europe; partition of India	**1947** *A Girl in Winter*	
		1948 Graham Greene, *The Heart of the Matter*

CHRONOLOGY

World events	Author's life	Literary events
		1949 Ivy Compton-Brunett, *Two Worlds and their Ways*; George Orwell, *Nineteen Eighty-four*
	1950 Becomes Sub-Librarian at the University of Belfast	
1951 Winston Churchill becomes British Prime Minister; Festival of Britain		**1951-75** Anthony Powell, *A Dance to the Music of Time*
1952 Death of George VI; accession of Elizabeth II		**1952** Samuel Beckett, *Waiting for Godot*
		1954 Iris Murdoch, *Under the Net*; William Golding, *Lord of the Flies*; Kingsley Amis, *Lucky Jim*; Dylan Thomas, *Under Milkwood*; Tennessee Williams, *Cat on a Hot Tin Roof*
1955 Anthony Eden becomes British Prime Minister; West Indian immigration to Britain increases	**1955** Becomes Librarian at the University of Hull; *The Less Deceived*	**1955** Kingsley Amis, *That Uncertain Feeling*
1956 Suez crisis; beginning of rock and roll music		**1956** John Osborne, *Look Back in Anger*
1957 Harold Macmillan becomes British Prime Minister; Wolfenden report on homosexuality and prostitution		**1957** Harold Pinter, *The Birthday Party*
		1958 Alan Sillitoe, *Saturday Night and Sunday Morning*, Samuel Beckett, *Krapp's Last Stand*
		1959 Alan Sillitoe, *The Loneliness of the Long-Distance Runner*; Arnold Wesker, *Roots*
1960 Macmillan makes 'Wind of Change' speech		**1960** Kingsley Amis, *Take a Girl Like You*; John Betjeman, *Summoned by Bells*

Chronology

World events	Author's life	Literary events
1961 Berlin Wall built		**1961** Samuel Beckett, *Happy Days*
1962 Commonwealth Immigrants Act passed to control numbers of immigrants; end of post-war National Service		**1962** Doris Lessing, *The Golden Notebook*; Anthony Burgess, *A Clockwork Orange*; Edith Sitwell, *The Outcasts*
1963 President Kennedy assassinated; Profumo scandal; Macmillan resigns; Alec Douglas-Home becomes British Prime Minister		**1963** John le Carré *The Spy Who Came in from the Cold*
1964 Harold Wilson becomes British Prime Minister; Commons vote to end Death Penalty	**1964** *The Whitsun Weddings*	**1964** John Osborne, *Inadmissible Evidence*; Samuel Beckett, *How It Is*; Joe Orton, *Entertaining Mr Sloane*
1965 Race Relations Act sets up Race Relations Board	**1965** Awarded the Queen's Gold Medal for Poetry	
1966 England wins World Cup		**1966** Graham Greene, *The Comedians*; Tom Stoppard, *Rosencrantz and Guildenstern Are Dead*
		1966–75 Paul Scott, *The Raj Quartet*
1967 Homosexual acts between consenting adults legalised in England and Wales		**1967** Ted Hughes, *Wodwo*; Joe Orton, *Loot*
1968 Enoch Powell's controversial speech on immigration		
1969 Legal age for right to vote reduced from 21 to 18; Divorce Reform Act makes breakdown of marriage cause for divorce; *Apollo 11* lands on the moon		**1969** W. H. Auden, *City Without Walls*; Joe Orton, *What the Butler Saw*; John Fowles, *The French Lieutenant's Woman*
1970 Edward Heath becomes British Prime Minister; many strikes in protest at Industrial Relations Bill; emergency power cuts	**1970** *All What Jazz: a record diary 1961–1968*	

CHRONOLOGY

World events	Author's life	Literary events
1971 Introduction of decimal currency; 'Angry Brigade' bombs home of Secretary of State for Employment		**1971** John Osborne, *West of Suez*
1972 Miners' strike; 'Bloody Sunday'; Britain joins the Common Market		
1973 Three Day Week introduced to save energy		**1973** Martin Amis, *The Rachel Papers*
1974 Harold Wilson becomes British Prime Minister; inflation reaches 16%	**1974** *High Windows*; awarded the CBE	**1974** John le Carré, *Tinker, Tailor, Soldier, Spy*; Philip Larkin, *High Windows*; Tom Stoppard, *Travesties*
1975 Inflation reaches 25%; Equal Opportunities Commission established; Margaret Thatcher becomes leader of the Conservative Party		
1976 Jim Callaghan becomes British Prime Minister		
1977 Aircraft and shipbuilding industries nationalised; Queen Elizabeth's Silver Jubilee	**1977** Chairs the Booker Prize panel	**1977** Martin Amis, *Dark Secrets*
	1978 Made Companion of Literature	
1979 Margaret Thatcher becomes Britain's first woman Prime Minister		**1979** Ted Hughes, *Moortown*; Harold Pinter, *Betrayal*; Caryl Churchill, *Cloud Nine*
1980 Unemployment more than 2 million		**1980** Iris Murdoch, *Nuns and Soldiers*
1981 Social Democratic Party is formed		**1981** John Osborne, *A Better Class of Person*; Samuel Beckett, *Ohio Impromptu*; Salman Rushdie, *Midnight's Children*

Chronology

World events	Author's life	Literary events
1982 Falkland Island Crisis		**1982** Malcolm Bradbury, *The After Dinner Game*; Caryl Churchill, *Top Girls*; Alan Bleasdale, *Boys from the Black Stuff*
1983 Sir Roy Griffiths's report, NHS Management Inquiry **1983 ON** Privitizations of British Telecom, British Gas, British Airways, British Petroleum; sale of council houses; reform of domestic rates into Community Charge (Poll Tax)		**1983** Fay Weldon, *The Life and Loves of a She-Devil*; Salman Rushdie, *Shame*
1984 IRA attack Conservative Party conference at Brighton **1984-5** Miner's strike	**1984** Receives an honorary D.Litt. from Oxford University	**1984** William Golding, *The Paper Men*; Tom Stoppard, *The Real Thing*; Julian Barnes, *Flaubert's Parrot*
	1985 Dies of cancer	**1985** Graham Swift, *Waterland*; Jeanette Winterson, *Oranges are not the Only Fruit*; Troy Kennedy Martin, *Edge of Darkness*
		1986 Iris Murdoch, *The Good Apprentice*; Graham Swift, *Learning to Swim and Other Stories*; Dennis Potter, *The Singing Detective*

LITERARY TERMS

absurdism an artistic movement of the twentieth century which showed humans existing in a meaningless and chaotic universe

alliteration a sequence of repeated consonantal sounds, most often at the beginnings of words or stressed syllables

allusion a passing reference in a work of literature to something outside itself; may include other works of literature, legend, historical facts, or autobiographical detail

aphorism a generally accepted principle of truth expressed in a short, pithy manner

apostrophe a rhetorical term for a speech addressed to a person, idea or thing

archaic ancient, old-fashioned

bathos a ludicrous descent from the elevated treatment of a subject to the ordinary and dull

choric relating to a chorus or repeated refrain

colloquial the kind of grammar and expression associated with everyday speech

end-stopped relates to a line of verse in which the end of the line coincides with an essential grammatical pause usually signalled by punctuation

epithet an adjective or adjectival phrase which defines a special quality or attribute

feminism a school of criticism which considers the role of gender in the creation or production of literature and in the reader's response to it

hiatus a gap, break or pause in an argument or action

iambic an iamb is a weak stress followed by a strong stress (ti-tum)

iambic pentameter a line of verse consisting of five iambic feet, the most common metre in English verse

image put simply, a 'word-picture'

imagery the use of 'word-pictures' in a description; may be the use of similes and metaphors or of qualities which appeal to the senses and the feelings

irony saying one thing while meaning another

lyrical relating to lyric poetry; a lyric is a (usually short) poem which expresses in a personal manner the feelings and thoughts of an individual speaker

LITERARY TERMS

jargon the technical language of any trade, profession or branch of scholarship

metaphor the description of something as being another thing

metaphysical relates to the philosophy of being and knowing but came to be associated with the so-called metaphysical poets of the seventeenth century, and their witty displays of ingenious comparisons, clever paradoxes and puns

modernism relates to the literature following the First World War, characterised by a quality of experimentalism and a self-conscious break from the artistic traditions and conventions that preceded it

paradox an apparently self-contradictory statement which yet contains a meaning or truth

pentameter a line of verse consisting of five metrical feet

parody (parodic) an imitation of a specific work or style devised so as to ridicule its characteristic features

pathos moments in works of art which evoke strong feelings of pity or sorrow are said to have this quality

persona a narrator who is not the author, or a first-person narrator constructed for a particular poetic purpose

postmodernism a vague term, fashionable in the 1980s, relating to the period immediately after modernism, when its experiments seemed to look familiar and even conventional. In general, post-modernism literature knowingly makes use of methods and motifs of former ages in the spirit of pastiche and eclecticism

post-structuralism a term covering the bundle of different approaches to language and literature, which holds that meaning is not inherent in words but depends upon their mutual relationships within the system of language

protagonist the leading character in a play, narrative or poem

psychoanalysis based on Freudian theory; a way of understanding human behaviour and culture in general, which holds that literature (like dreams) is the expression of repressed subconscious desires

quatrain a stanza consisting of four lines

Literary Terms

Restoration the forty-year period after the restoration of the monarchy in England in 1660, whose literature was characterised chiefly by wit and satire

Romanticism a vague term, but chiefly characterised by: a value placed on emotion rather than reason; an interest in nature and the self; imagination and symbolism; and rebellion against both poetic conventions and political institutions. Romanticism is usually defined as the period dating from 1789 (the French Revolution) to about 1830.

symbol something which represents something else (often an idea or quality) by analogy or association

syntax (syntactic) the arrangement of terms in their appropriate forms and proper order, in order to achieve meaning

stereotype a standard fixed idea; may indicate a cliché (an ordinary perception made dull by repetition) or signify the stock characters, ideas and situations that are the typical material of literature

tetrameter a line of verse consisting of four feet

trimeter a line of verse consisting of three feet

Author of this note

David Punter is Professor of English and Graduate Dean of Arts at the University of Bristol. Among his many books are *The Literature of Terror* (2 vols, 1996), *Writing the Passions* (2000) and *Postcolonial Imaginings: Fictions of a New World Order* (2000).

Notes

Advanced Level Titles

York Notes Advanced

Margaret Atwood
Cat's Eye

Margaret Atwood
The Handmaid's Tale

Jane Austen
Emma

Jane Austen
Mansfield Park

Jane Austen
Persuasion

Jane Austen
Pride and Prejudice

Jane Austen
Sense and Sensibility

Alan Bennett
Talking Heads

William Blake
Songs of Innocence and of Experience

Charlotte Brontë
Jane Eyre

Charlotte Brontë
Villette

Emily Brontë
Wuthering Heights

Angela Carter
Nights at the Circus

Geoffrey Chaucer
The Franklin's Prologue and Tale

Geoffrey Chaucer
The Miller's Prologue and Tale

Geoffrey Chaucer
Prologue to the Canterbury Tales

Geoffrey Chaucer
The Wife of Bath's Prologue and Tale

Samuel Taylor Coleridge
Selected Poems

Joseph Conrad
Heart of Darkness

Daniel Defoe
Moll Flanders

Charles Dickens
Bleak House

Charles Dickens
Great Expectations

Charles Dickens
Hard Times

Emily Dickinson
Selected Poems

John Donne
Selected Poems

Carol Ann Duffy
Selected Poems

George Eliot
Middlemarch

George Eliot
The Mill on the Floss

T.S. Eliot
Selected Poems

T.S. Eliot
The Waste Land

F. Scott Fitzgerald
The Great Gatsby

E.M. Forster
A Passage to India

Brian Friel
Translations

Thomas Hardy
Jude the Obscure

Thomas Hardy
The Mayor of Casterbridge

Thomas Hardy
The Return of the Native

Thomas Hardy
Selected Poems

Thomas Hardy
Tess of the d'Urbervilles

Seamus Heaney
Selected Poems from Opened Ground

Nathaniel Hawthorne
The Scarlet Letter

Homer
The Iliad

Homer
The Odyssey

Aldous Huxley
Brave New World

Kazuo Ishiguro
The Remains of the Day

Ben Jonson
The Alchemist

James Joyce
Dubliners

John Keats
Selected Poems

Christopher Marlowe
Doctor Faustus

Christopher Marlowe
Edward II

Arthur Miller
Death of a Salesman

John Milton
Paradise Lost Books I & II

Toni Morrison
Beloved

George Orwell
Nineteen-Eighty-Four

Sylvia Plath
Selected Poems

Alexander Pope
Rape of the Lock and other poems

William Shakespeare
Antony and Cleopatra

William Shakespeare
As You Like It

William Shakespeare
Hamlet

William Shakespeare
King Lear

William Shakespeare
Macbeth

William Shakespeare
Measure for Measure

William Shakespeare
The Merchant of Venice

William Shakespeare
A Midsummer Night's Dream

William Shakespeare
Much Ado About Nothing

William Shakespeare
Othello

William Shakespeare
Richard II

William Shakespeare
Richard III

William Shakespeare
Romeo and Juliet

William Shakespeare
The Taming of the Shrew

Advanced Level Titles (Continued)

William Shakespeare
The Tempest

William Shakespeare
Twelfth Night

William Shakespeare
The Winter's Tale

George Bernard Shaw
Saint Joan

Mary Shelley
Frankenstein

Jonathan Swift
Gulliver's Travels and A Modest Proposal

Alfred, Lord Tennyson
Selected Poems

Virgil
The Aeneid

Alice Walker
The Color Purple

Oscar Wilde
The Importance of Being Earnest

Tennessee Williams
A Streetcar Named Desire

Jeanette Winterson
Oranges Are Not the Only Fruit

John Webster
The Duchess of Malfi

Virginia Woolf
To the Lighthouse

W.B. Yeats
Selected Poems

Metaphysical Poets

Other Titles

GCSE and equivalent levels

Maya Angelou
I Know Why the Caged Bird Sings

Jane Austen
Pride and Prejudice

Alan Ayckbourn
Absent Friends

Elizabeth Barrett Browning
Select Poems

Robert Bolt
A Man for All Seasons

Harold Brighouse
Hobson's Choice

Charlotte Brontë
Jane Eyre

Emily Brontë
Wuthering Heights

Shelagh Delaney
A Taste of Honey

Charles Dickens
David Copperfield

Charles Dickens
Great Expectations

Charles Dickens
Hard Times

Charles Dickens
Oliver Twist

Roddy Doyle
Paddy Clarke Ha Ha Ha

George Eliot
Silas Marner

George Eliot
The Mill on the Floss

Anne Frank
The Diary of Anne Frank

William Golding
Lord of the Flies

Oliver Goldsmith
She Stoops to Conquer

Willis Hall
The Long and the Short and the Tall

Thomas Hardy
Far from the Madding Crowd

Thomas Hardy
The Mayor of Casterbridge

Thomas Hardy
Tess of the d'Urbervilles

Thomas Hardy
The Withered Arm and other Wessex Tales

L.P. Hartley
The Go-Between

Seamus Heaney
Selected Poems

Susan Hill
I'm the King of the Castle

Barry Hines
A Kestrel for a Knave

Louise Lawrence
Children of the Dust

Harper Lee
To Kill a Mockingbird

Laurie Lee
Cider with Rosie

Arthur Miller
The Crucible

Arthur Miller
A View from the Bridge

Robert O'Brien
Z for Zachariah

Frank O'Connor
My Oedipus Complex and Other Stories

George Orwell
Animal Farm

J.B. Priestley
An Inspector Calls

J.B. Priestley
When We Are Married

Willy Russell
Educating Rita

Willy Russell
Our Day Out

J.D. Salinger
The Catcher in the Rye

William Shakespeare
Henry IV Part 1

William Shakespeare
Henry V

William Shakespeare
Julius Caesar

William Shakespeare
Macbeth

William Shakespeare
The Merchant of Venice

William Shakespeare
A Midsummer Night's Dream

William Shakespeare
Much Ado About Nothing

William Shakespeare
Romeo and Juliet

William Shakespeare
The Tempest

William Shakespeare
Twelfth Night

George Bernard Shaw
Pygmalion

Mary Shelley
Frankenstein

R.C. Sherriff
Journey's End

Rukshana Smith
Salt on the Snow

John Steinbeck
Of Mice and Men

Robert Louis Stevenson
Dr Jekyll and Mr Hyde

Jonathan Swift
Gulliver's Travels

Robert Swindells
Daz 4 Zoe

Mildred D. Taylor
Roll of Thunder, Hear My Cry

Mark Twain
Huckleberry Finn

James Watson
Talking in Whispers

Edith Wharton
Ethan Frome

William Wordsworth
Selected Poems

A Choice of Poets

Mystery Stories of the Nineteenth Century including The Signalman

Nineteenth Century Short Stories

Poetry of the First World War

Six Women Poets